"Loving Who You Are and Being Loved in It"

A Pastor's Wife Memoir

Judah Moore

Scriptures marked KJV are taken from the Holy Bible, King James Version, Copyright © 1972 by Thomas Nelson Inc., Camden, New Jersey 08103.

ISBN: 979-8-9865807-1-5

Library of Congress Control Number: 2022913722

Cover Design & Illustration: by Kozakura @Fiverr

Visionary Cover Artist: Judah Moore

Published by: G Publishing LLC

Printed in the U.S.A.

TABLE OF CONTENTS

DEDICATION

To my precious three adult millennials. You are my dearest loved ones. Visions of you within my heart helped to guide you in each stage of encouraging your spirit as we successfully progressed through life in our journey together. God loves you. I am thankful to God for blessing me to be your mother. Always let the light of Jesus Christ's love to shine brightly within you.

<div align="center">~~~</div>

I would like to dedicate this book to all the pastor wives who have loved and given their all in their marriages. I pray that after you finish this book, your hearts will be healed. I hope that my experience gives you hope and inspiration to become everything your heart desires. I pray that you will continue to walk more graciously with your Heavenly Father and love yourself where you have been wounded. You are lovely; keep loving who you are and being loved in it.

<div align="center">~~~</div>

FOREWORD

Robin K. Cage

Loving Who You Are and Being Loved in It, what a purposeful title, written by a very purposeful Woman.

When asked to pen this, my mind was suddenly flooded with memories of Judy and me as children. We looked alike; acted like sisters, we even sound alike when speaking at times. She is a dear relative and my very close friend. You see, Judy as I call her, had this uncanny ability to access my mood. She was always so sensitive to it! I lived about two hours away, and her family would often come and spend the weekend at our home. We would travel to her location and do the same. She was five years old when we first met, and I was eight. We were inseparable. As the years evolved, we did also. Marriage, the birth of our children, the breakups, and divorces, hers and my own. We have always shared lives parallel to one another. We were close as children and have remained close for 60 years.

We grew up in a time when you wrote letters and mailed them to one another. We would share the most heartfelt sentiments during our written communications. Judy has continued that gift by writing this book for all of you. Through the ups and downs of relationships, I have watched her grow in grace and wisdom. I have witnessed an elegant strength and tenacity in her character that only God can grant and solidify. She is gifted with an innate sensitivity that can be described as gentle and kind; yet honest and right. You may leave in your feelings, nonetheless, you will know that everything she shared with you, about You, was true.

We have shared testimonies about our lives that will follow us to our graves. No one can unlock those confidences. That is how private and protective she has always been of me, and of her. I can trust her with my secrets, and that has always been something I have cherished, the evidence of her strength and character. Beautifully saved and boldly holding fast to her faith, her commitment to God is unshakable, so is her love for her children and family. Raising three beautiful children as a single/divorcee' and the sacrifice it took, she was blessed to be rewarded with a beautiful marriage to her late husband.

Isaiah 61:3 says, *"To appoint unto them that mourn in Zion, to give unto them beauty for ashes, the oil of joy for mourning, the garment of praise for the spirit of heaviness: that they might be called trees of righteousness, the planting of the LORD, that he might be glorified."* Judy is one of those trees.

If you need encouragement, read "Loving Who You Are and Being Loved in It," as it is written from a place of pain and triumph over the enemy. I prayerfully encourage you to read with the anticipation of knowing that you too can find the love that God so richly has assigned to your heart and your life.

Robin K. Cage
Freelance Beauty & Image Consultant

"For I know the plans I have for you," declares the Lord, plans to prosper you and not to harm you, plans to give you hope and a future. Then you will call on me and come and pray to me, and I will listen to you."

Jeremiah 29:11-12

New International Version

PREFACE

From the beginning of my journey until I was finally absorbed into the fullness of my experience, I kept a paper trail of short stories. Nonetheless, I knew one day I would write my own memoir. I remember keeping several diaries as a junior in high school, expressing my disappointments, emotions, and love secrets; and when I worked in a convalescent home during the summers while in high school, I began writing poetry. Their frailty and inability to care for themselves as elder people provided me with the opportunity to get to know them personally and how productive they were throughout their lifetime. Nobody ever expects to experience life-changing events. The one thing that mattered in their new life was how the world perceived their weakness and inability to make decisions about their well-being. Their opinion was no longer valued. It did not matter who they were before they got older. They were estranged. There were only a few families who adored and loved them. There were few employees who enjoyed caring for them.

Loving Who You Are and Being Loved in It is an internal struggle to stay relatable amid our setback, no matter how much you are hurting. You have a voice. You are somebody to someone. Someone loves and appreciates you, but you must first love yourself. Loving yourself ensures you are existent and purposeful. The enemy wants us to be caught up with its reality, and not in Christ's heart toward us. When your focus is on God you can drown out the nay-sayer. The nay-sayer that wants you to look at its world, as it is written in the Book of Matthew 4:1-11. *Loving Who You Are* fortifies you and gives you the strength to break every bond and stronghold that tries to snatch you at its will. If you are a pastor's wife who sometimes feels alone; a single mother doing her best to provide for her children without the financial means to adequately provide her children; or a woman who tries to be submissive to her husband but instead is used as a punching bag ... there are people who love, you. Some strong-willed women are not valued as a helpmate, a partner, a confidante, or friend. You have a mission, a purpose, and a destiny. My experience was unexpected. I did not see it coming. I had never thought my life would have an emotional and adverse effect of me. It was life altering. Life-changing. I had a life with goals that was abrupted, but the interruption of those expectancy's left me feeling froze ... pulling me away into isolation where it thought it would torture me, and by "it" within the lines, I'm referring to the enemy.

For far too long, I have kept this nuisance and obsessed secret of my personal journey from others. I could not get away from the thought of not writing about what I'd been through because it would have made my living phony, and I'm not a fan of phoniness. If I had given in to the idea of remaining quiet and pretending, my life's purpose would have been branded as "I got another one fooled." Well, the enemy is a liar. I have always known God had a true purpose for my life as a child, but the enemy always got in the way. Now that I know that I know, I can walk in the peace of God. But know this: reliving my experience was far from easy. I call it my wilderness experience as I trek through the sands absorbing the torture of emotional pains. Days, if not months, would pass by before I could return to pecking away on my keyboard to complete this book, simply because I did not want to hurt anymore. I could not bear reliving what I had experienced over twenty odds years in the wilderness. The enemy was trying to destroy me. But I fought back.

Every ounce of me fought back. When I wanted to give up my mind stayed on the prize, and the prize were my children.

I began to understand God's plan as I progressed through each episodic journey. I was progressing. I was getting healed. This is the true story of how God shielded me from the enemy. The enemy wishes for God's chosen to avoid the presence and peace of our Heavenly Father by leading us to 'it's' false promises, which keep us blind to our destiny. The enemy gains power only through what a person negatively succumbs to. Therefore, place all your trust and faith in God.

I was not used as a punching bag, but my past life as a pastor's wife felt like I had been punched. I never imagined myself marrying or being divorced by a pastor. There were no forewarning signs that this was going to happen. The scope of our family unit changed everything, and it was something I was trying to avoid: a dysfunctional marriage. As pastor wives it is vitally important to keep spouses in prayer. I am not alluding to that I never prayed for my ex-spouse, but he was his own person, an individual in ministry who needed to get out of his own way so that God could have His way; and this applies for us all. Not only was I concerned about our family, but also about the church, our members, and those who trusted us to give them the Word of God when we fellowshipped. Churches, no doubt, try to keep their congregations together after a divorce, but how can a house divided stand when the leader(s) fall? It requires a lot of soul searching, fasting, praying, and repenting to restore the body of Christ. A church split, and repairing a mistake is never the same, yet *"Our God is able to do exceedingly, abundantly above all we ask or think"* (Ephesians 3:20, KJV). The enemy despises the church (being and within us) and the gathering of saints to worship (being one voice in us) in the body of Christ, as the truth of God's Word is spoken into us (being corporately), reviving, activating, and invigorating our faith to soar toward our intentions to truly magnify the Lord.

George Barna, President, and Founder of Barna Research Group commented on the family indicates:

"While learning that born-again Christians are more likely than others to divorce may be upsetting, this pattern has long existed. Even more troubling, many of those who divorce believe their faith community rejects them rather than supports and heals them. The study calls into question the efficacy with which churches minister to families. The husband and wife bear ultimate responsibility for their marriage, nevertheless, the high divorce rate among Christians calls the assumption that churches provide truly practical and life-changing support for marriages into question."

Divorce effects the very core of our lives. While I was attending seminary facing the separation from my children and a divorce from their father, my schoolmate asked me, "which feels more like a death, getting a divorce or losing a loved one?" I thought about it and analyzed both scenarios. I had commented to her "a divorce feels more like a death to me because you are still communicating with that individual or have an idea they are around, and if you have children, you still have something in common with them no matter how you feel toward that person." She agreed. As we take passage through a divorce, we realize we are stronger than we were before because we learned to take on the challenges and learn from them. This gives us our own identity. A new identity. More confidence and an appreciation for life. We can evolve even further if we choose to live right seeking God's face.

When I provided spiritual marital counseling to divorcees and married couples, my hope was always to reunite the couples; or to help a divorcee rediscover her unique identity that was embedded within her. And as you research the titles, you will notice that they're divided into three sections because they're clearly related to my journey and a brief adventure throughout certain periods of my life.

It is my hope that as you read about my unwavering existence as a pastor's wife, a single-divorced mother, and a resolute servant to Christ, that the layers of my roles will deepen your relationship and calling with God. It was my intention to share my experiences to provide healing for those who may have gone through what I encountered being a pastor's wife.

According to the statistical data from The National Healthy Marriage Resource Center (NHMRC) translate that:

"As African American married mothers who attend church are 31% more likely to report having excellent relationships with their husbands, an additional 50% of their marriages will end in divorce. (Let me interject based on my research was no data recorded for 1995 and 1996 during my divorce). Nonetheless, the divorce rate remained stable at four divorces for every 1,000 Americans," and there has been a steady decline within the same percentile up to 2019. Most pastor wives' emotional and psychological happiness while being married to spouses in ministry, indicates that 80% feel left out and unappreciated by church members; 56% say they have no close friends in the church, and 60% expressed a desire to further their training so they could serve better; 80% reported feeling pressured to do things and be someone they are not in church. 80% of spouses believe their spouse is overworked; 80% of pastors wish their spouse would pursue a different career, and another 80% believe they spend insufficient time with their spouse."

As you can see, the work of the ministry is demanding work, but if everyone loves one another as Jesus commanded, the entire body of Christ would be joyous and free.

Finally, our Heavenly Father will put us all to the test. It does not mean He doesn't care about you. It means He has something better in store for you and wants to prepare you so you can grow in His Word and know His voice. If I ever must travel through a wilderness again, I will know that I am protected because my God has been with me.

INTRODUCTION

~~~

Moving toward our thirteenth wedding anniversary, God showed me in a dream a desert without footprints, and my walking eastward on the hot sands with a few faithful friends from our church ministry. In the stretch of the distance, I hazily saw the image of three large camels and three statues, resembling physical bodies standing in a postured position waiting for my arrival. As I walked closer, the camels were lying comfortably on the hot sand, draped with expensive apparel over their faces and body, and in between their massive humps were drapery of textiles, beautiful linen, water canteens, and silk pillows. As I drew nearer to them even closer to them, their massive built and physical physique resembled the image of their strength. These camels had been assigned just for me, but not only that, for my children to ensure they were comfortable for what seemed like an exceptionally long journey ahead. The statuette-like bodies turned out to be men dressed in an article of clothing of an Egyptian style attire. They assisted my friends who were with me in saddling up my two sons and daughter ages 10, 7, and 5 upon their respective camels. One of the men then handed me one by one three long thick leather straps to pull, gauge, and guide our direction onward, as I walked through the desert imprinting my footsteps in the sands that now was my wilderness experience.

Now, this is how the dream unfolds through my life journey …
~~~

CHAPTER ONE

"Loving Who You Are ..."

"For I know the thoughts that I think toward you, saith the LORD, thoughts of peace, and not of evil, to give you an expected end."
Jeremiah 29:11 (KJV)

~~~

The Dream

In the days to come, I pondered on that dream. I searched within my spirit for the interpretation. I knew at some point God would share with me the meaning. I meditated on it so hard in the days forward that I decided to bypass it and just wait patiently for God to speak to me. One day out of the clear blue, and without hesitation, I had spoken with my sister about spending time with her one weekend at her new house. I never imagined I was headed for a turn of events that would take on an emotional and traumatic change in my life. Out of nowhere, completely, and unexpectedly, the understanding and interpretation of my dream displayed an act of utter disbelief.

But before we get into the life of the story, I want to reveal how I met my husband at the time before he became my ex-spouse.

I had a close friend who worked at the same hospital where I worked. She worked in the Pathology Department, and I worked in Psychiatry as an Emergency Room Secretary. She always provided me with spiritual knowledge. I was not born again at the time. I was a young party girl exploring a new life apart from my first husband
~~~

after a recent divorce. I was celebrating my freedom as a single lady with no children. I was making good money. I had my car and lived with my parents temporarily. No one could stand in the way of my freedom. My close friend in the Pathology Department came to work one day and shared with me how she and another friend went to Toledo, Ohio for a church service. She was overly excited and happy about her visit and encouraged me to come along. I was not interested in traveling a long distance to attend church. She kept at me every week to come to church with her. Finally, I agreed. I had given her the address of my parents' house. And here comes the day. A tremendously hot scorching summer day. Now my family and relatives know how I am about being hot. My relatives would tease me about it all the time. I did not like being hot or around anyone until I could find a cool place to gather myself. I had worked a double shift in the week, and Saturday was going to be my day to sleep. My friend comes over to my house to get me. I heard my mom say, "Judy, I think you've got company." I thought to myself, oh no, not today. I tried to convince my mom to tell my friend I was not feeling well today. Well, my mom was not having it! My mom was so impressed with my friend. I had never seen or heard my mom act the way she did. She was floating around like a butterfly and laughing with so much joy. She came back into the bedroom and said, "get up." "You're going to church today." I tried to convince my mom again to tell my friend I was sick, but she was annoyingly persistent to get me up. Again, I had never seen her act like this before. I know when I was seven or eight, mom would dress us up to go to this corner church adjacent to our house. As a few years passed, I found myself going to church by myself, asking my mom to come with me, but for some reason, she was hesitant to attend. I attended that

                                              Judah Moore

church for almost three or four years until the family church moved away. They eventually developed several mega-churches and grew enormously. I had glimpsed back to those days when my mom looked sad and troubled as I left the house to go to church, which made me get up to get dressed for the long ride to Toledo, Ohio.

As I was getting ready, I could hear my mom and my close friend chattering it up in the living room. The sun was beaming so brightly. My friend had a beautiful caring personality resembling the same brightness of the sun. It was like she was a special angel sent to me. As I recalled, my close friend was not the first person who had come by in my life to invite me to their churches. I could hear my friend talking about her church visit to Toledo with my mom, and how she had been anxious to take me with her to visit. My mom had such a sweet-sounding lightness to her voice. She normally liked all my friends, but this one was exceptional. She yelled, "Judy, you ready?" She came into the bedroom to get me, as I was finishing up. I was finally ready for an hour's ride to Ohio. I greeted my friend and kissed my mom goodbye. As we walked toward the car, there was her friend, who would become a close confidant and leader in our church, who would bring seasoned women in the gospel who would take me under their wing for a season. But for now, at that moment, I looked at her car. I knew I was going to be extremely uncomfortable. It was small, and she had no air conditioning. She laughed about her car as we were introduced, which was unbelievable to me. All I could think about was being even hotter.

My hair was long at the time flying all around my face; this way and that way while sitting in the back seat of her car. I was trying to keep my composure and not complain. I could hear them talking and enjoying themselves in the front seat but decided to remain quiet because I would only be yelling and repeating myself due to the forced air engulfing the car. I just could not wait to get out of the car and into a cool place. When we arrived at the church, I prayed that they would have air conditioning. As we arrived, the church was small and on acres of land. We were in the middle of nowhere, but surely as we walked inside, I felt a cool breeze. The church was filled with women and small children. The pastor sang and preached a good sermon. After service, I thought we would be driving directly back to Michigan, but instead, the pastor invited many of the church members and friends over to have dinner at the mother's house. I thought what a kind gesture. The home had numerous fans, which was perfect. We all sat around the table and had Kentucky Fried Chicken with all the sides. There were about ten of us present. Afterward, some excused themselves and went into the living room and some of us were still eating. I eventually found a seat in this big house and listened to all the conversations. It was a refreshing moment to hear how everyone felt comfortable with each other laughing and joking around. At one point a two-way conversation developed just between the pastor and me after I had made comment to the group. We had a lot in common, I thought. I was making some of the people in the room uncomfortable, so I got up and went outside with the deacon and a few other people and lit up a cigarette. Suddenly, everyone looked at me. Everyone on the porch was appalled as they showed their disgust and shame toward me. I did not find any harm in what I had done. I was outside and not inside the house. They were preaching and pointing their fingers at me and shaking their heads. I thought about how it may have offended them, so I kindly put the cigarette

                                                          Judah Moore

out. After all, we were at the residence of the Church Mother's home. I was in my mid-twenties and only thinking about myself. I was thankful the mother did not come outside to give me a tongue lashing or spank my hands or tell me off. You know our elders spoke plainly back then, and I understand why.

The pastor came outside to find out what the commotion was all about. When they start telling him what I did, I was expecting a speech, a rebuke, a scolding, another look of disgust like they gave me … but no, it was not that way at all. Instead, he had compassion and understood my addiction to cigarettes. I had been smoking since 14, and I was hooked. He was slow to respond to my accusers. And he said something that paraphrased what Jesus had said to the women who had committed adultery, *"So when they continued asking him, he lifted up himself, and said unto them, He that is without sin among you, let him first cast a stone at her." (John 8:7, KJV).* From there everyone who thought I would be embarrassed by the pastor's chastisement disbursed and said nothing more about my smoking. He gave me an out and looked at me and said if you want to smoke, smoke … and at that point, I knew that my life could be changed. My life of troubles stared me right back in my face. I had been convicted and I had no problem with it. I saw that I had no direction. I had been away from church since my teens, and the developmental growing pains of family dysfunctions had inundated my soul. I stood pondering on the scripture I had never heard before. Yet, it nurtured me while standing there outside on the porch. I knew in that instance that my lifestyle choices had to come to an end. I thought to myself, maybe I will join this church and become a member too.

My midnight work schedule had not allowed me to have weekends off, so the pastor would call and check on me. I found myself communicating often with him and we eventually became close over time. I continued to go to Ohio when my schedule allowed, but it was few and in between. My close friend traveled with me a few times but eventually stopped attending church. A few months flew by, and I discovered she was in the hospital on the day I recommitted my life to the Lord. When we went to visit her, I noticed her spark was dim, but she was glad to see me. I told her all the exciting news about my giving my life to the Lord and how free I felt. She said, "I can tell, you have such a glow about you." We stayed and talked with her for a while, but for some reason, she seemed so sad, but, happy for me. I tried cheering her up. It helped a little. After we visited with her that day, I was unable to attend church again due to scheduling, so one weekend the pastor drove to Michigan to see about me. We grew closer at that point and were married within five months. Over time, we started a church in Michigan and stayed with my relatives until we found a house. At some point, my close friend disappeared. She was no longer an employee at the hospital where we both worked. When I went to her department, her co-workers told me she no longer worked with them. I tried calling her on several occasions, but no answer. I inquired about her by asking another friend of hers if she had seen or heard from her, and she indicated she had not seen or heard from her in weeks. It was strange to me that she had suddenly disappeared.

After our marriage, we had a strong ministry of people who loved God and who wanted to serve faithfully in both locations, Michigan, and Ohio. I was a newborn baby Christian. My observations of these mature saints taught me how to praise God when I was ashamed to lift my hands or dance for joy. They had taught me how to live a Christian life. I had some who would come to our home and have bible study with me. I felt intimidated by their knowledge, but I was eager to learn and studied God's ways. I grew even more. After the birth of our first son, I began to minister. My spiritual mentor who drove the small car to Ohio was connected to a few powerful women in their ministry who operated in their gifts and their calling fully and unapologetically. I was amazed and intimated by their humility and love for Christ as they allowed God to use them. I always wanted to be in their presence, no matter how uncomfortable I felt. I wanted what God wanted me to have as they shared their stories, and through my studies, God shared with me His interpretation of the Word. Within years we began to flourish in our immediate family, our network with other church congregations and gaining momentum as a body of Christ. My being absent from church, however, after the birth of our two children plus staying at home with them for a six-week duration and returning to our church was a mess. I sensed it. There was a change in the atmosphere, and it was not getting better. I was always putting out fires. There were new people (mostly women) attending the church who I did not know or hear about, and when I returned, I embraced them with open arms. Call it spiritual intuition, as a pastor's wife she knows when other women in the church want to covet your blessings, your spouse, and your children. But more importantly, a pastor's wife must make sure it's not their own insecurities involved in causing the discord within the church and running people away. I can honestly say, I had my fair share of slaying and praying and asking if they were sent by God that they would be a blessing to the ministry; and if not bless them to be used elsewhere. A few stayed, and others began to dwindle away from the church as I recouped and regained my strength after giving birth. When you seek God for protection over your family and the church, He will show you whose intentions are pure and impure. I did win some souls through prayer as they had a heart of conviction and recognized they were being used to try to destroy the ministry but over time, I discovered the women were being enticed. Too often my spouse would be on calls chatting away with women from the church, especially those who were just getting to the church. Too often he had women visitors come to our home without asking my permission. They would be there without my knowledge while I was tending to our children or running errands. Some had left the church because as they began to know me, they felt guilty in some way and broke away from the church. They were apologetic, and I forgave them. To my knowledge, they had not slept with my husband. In turn, some became angry with my spouse, and he began to blame me for their leaving.

My husband was committing various forms of intense emotional intimacy with other women in the church. I was fighting a losing battle. The emotional stress of it all was wearing me down to the point I felt myself becoming sick in my body. I remembered the days when we did enjoy each other, but suddenly he just seemed like he did not care about us. I always encouraged us to go out to dinner, breakfast, or to a movie. He always complained about finances when we had the finances to do something. It did not matter to me where we went, it was needful for our marriage to thrive. Once the ministry started to grow, I noticed him changing more. We did not have an outreach program, but somehow our church started to fill up increasingly each week. I would encourage us to sing together as we once did when we started our church, or even preach a sermon together to show that we were on one accord despite our differences. His messages were becoming manipulative, calculating, and scheming; and when I tried to critique him on his messages and questioned his intentions an argument would ensue. My entire family (my mother, my aunt, cousin, and siblings) eventually left the church because they did not enjoy the sermons and other matters of the heart, which they did not want to share with me. He had become a completely different person over the 12 years of our marriage.

One day, as I was passing by our church building, I noticed his car was parked out front. There was another car parked behind him. As I circled the block, parked, walked up the stairs, and opened the door, I observed him and another female member moving my seat off from the pulpit area. They weren't aware I was standing there listening as they chatted about how they were going to place my chair. I just watched them both. They were in a serious conversation about deciding where to move the chair. She picked it up and moved it over toward my office door, far from the pulpit. He remarked to her with a nod. I said to them, "what are you doing?" They both froze and turned around to look at me. I could see the evidence of betrayal on both of their faces. They tried to explain their reasoning for moving one chair. My spouse was determined to stand his ground and not express any sensitivity or heartfelt apology to his wife, as I looked at him. I said, "you know what, this is perfect. I like where my chair is placed." Still, this let me know where I stood with him and how he did not appreciate the gift that God gave him. There were a lot of things changing in the church that I was not aware of which explained this incident. I had never felt this way before, but I started to feel I was being ostracized and separated from the people during our services. Over a fleeting time, there was an even more appreciation and closeness from the congregation towards me. I also noticed how clearly; I was able to hear the voice of the Lord from my new sitting location. Over and away from the pulpit, God was molding and shaping me within, and I could feel the positive changes and enjoyed being in my special place in the church where I could hear God speak with me.

In my eyes, our home and the church were not my sacred place. I was experiencing more chaos at home as people were over from the church five days a week, eight hours a day doing this and doing that for him. I had decided to homeschool our children and eventually enrolled them in preschool and elementary school as I attained a certificate. I could not manage to care for my children properly with all the interruptions throughout the day and week. I did not understand the reasoning behind what he was doing. If we were operating as a normal family, we would have been more successful in our endeavors by spending time with our children promoting a solid foundation in our relationship as we continue in the work which God was preparing us for. When I encouraged us again to take a ride or go somewhere to have a meal, it was always "how can we go out, when the church people can't even go out or do things with their family?" I found no reasoning for his explanation as it did not make sense, because if the messages were of faith and trust there would not be an issue. How can the church body walk in faith, when there was no faith in us as one? It was obvious, that the people were more important to him than me, and his children.

I returned to college to finish my bachelor's degree, and after graduating, my instructor advised me to immediately enroll in seminary school. She had already made plans with the Dean and had discussed them with me. When I told my husband that I was going to get my master's degree in pastoral counseling solely to minister to women at our church, he seemed to approve even more. Yet, after some time when I was studying and drafting papers, he became unsettled. I had planned for my children to be cared for which was not an inconvenience because I had enrolled in night classes. But the arguments ensued increasingly because I was consumed with moving ahead wanting to do something worthwhile with my life. And all the while, I was still capable of giving my children all they needed. To my surprise one day while I was studying, my spouse insinuated that I thought I was better than him. I could not believe he felt this way. This made it clear that he was growing increasingly jealous of his own wife.

Wilderness Journey

On October 14, 1996, I was hit with a ton of bricks. Coming home from my evening class as I was entering my last year in school, my husband, and the father of our three children met me at the door and asked that I come in and sit down so that we could talk. I laid my purse and books down and sat down calmly thinking the subject would be related to someone in the church. He told me emphatically with a straight face, "God said, you are no longer my wife." I looked at him in disbelief, shocked, stunned, and said boldly with a loud voice, "God didn't tell you that!" "Whatever it is, we can make this work," because I believed we could. I thought he was going on his mixed feelings from our last conversation regarding school, but now I sensed it was deeper than that. I said, "God does not like divorce!" I had seen from his posture and the glaring at me that he meant what he said and that he believed that God told him this insidious lie. No matter how I voiced my concern it did not matter. The man who told me when we first met, "God said you are to be my wife," now received a different message from God. His 'own' decision and discussion concerning our marriage were short-lived in his mind. He told me I had to leave the house immediately and recommended that I go and stay with my sister. I went to gather my things and move toward the side door from the breezeway to go inside the house to talk with my children, but he told me it would be best that I do not see our children, and to just leave the house. I thought about the request not to see my children before leaving and agreed with myself to avoid the unknown.

I turned the knob, and the door closed immediately behind me. I quietly stood outside. I felt the coldness in the air after just leaving a deceitful person, a role model, a figure, and the character of a man who claimed to be a man of God. A cold chill blew across my face, to my hands, and down my back. The wind felt different. There was a strange quietness and stillness in the air as I looked up at that dark blue sky reflecting from the stars … contemplating and going over in my mind what just happened, I was in a daze. I thought I had been removed from that ole feeling of not being wanted stemming from my illegitimacy as a child. It was just a meditative thought as I stood there motionless. I felt God's anger and disapproval of this situation. All I could do was fix my eyes on the heavens seeking His direction. My thoughts were preoccupied and filled with the well-being of my precious children, and what they would think about not having or seeing their mother caring for them tonight, or even in the morning. How will they sleep without me? I had

                                        Judah Moore

so many thoughts running through my mind concerning my children, that I felt myself slowly falling apart emotionally. The more my emotions surfaced, the more I wanted to react with retaliation, but I heard the voice of God speak to me saying, "You've got to be strong, your children are going to need you, move forward." I was trying to hold back my tears, and yet I heeded the voice of the Lord, and quietly said within myself, 'Yes Lord. I must move now!'

It was getting close to midnight. I needed to find somewhere to stay. Even though the children's father recommended that I stay with my sister, I recalled the conversation I had with her a month or two ago and headed to the other side of the city to visit her unexpectedly. I was not able to recall whether I called her in advance, but it only took a knock on her door, to receive a welcoming embrace.

As I walked into her large Tudor home, she was discussing the bedroom and where I could sleep. I did not want to talk much and went straight upstairs and laid across the bed thinking about the whole ordeal. I knew my sister would understand my disappearance suddenly, and more importantly, I knew she would be there to listen when I was ready to talk. It was difficult for me to sleep. I pondered on how I was going to manage the many phases and facets of living without my children, and my not being in an environment that I was so familiar with. My children would be unable to stay with me due to the distances of my travel taking them back and forth to school, plus my being in school. The added stress of facing all my classmates would be a challenge because we were all close and supportive of each other. We worked in groups on didactical studies to build our counseling skills often sharing our personal issues. Facing my immediate problem of sorrow would draw unwanted attention to myself throughout the school, and even a nervous breakdown. I was trying to keep it together even as my mind was racing. It was too much for me to manage and gauge a directive approach. I needed to find my footing. I did not have a confidant or know a person trustworthy enough to whom I was willing to entrust, or even expose what I was going through. I have always worked out my life dilemmas on my own. All my close lady friends were in our church. They knew me. They knew how to pray, and if I asked, they were on it. They knew my spirit. They cared about me. However, despite all my strength I would need to intentionally keep myself away from too much intimate personal contact with my peers, just so I could manage my emotions and thoughts. I did not want to be pitied, nor did I want anyone prying into my personal affairs. It was bad enough that I was experiencing so much emotional shame. I did not want anyone pointing their fingers at me and asking if I was alright. I had to stay strong for my children.

As I faced the few days ahead, my maternal instinct and love kicked into high gear only to realize I was being forbidden to see my children. On the first Sunday after my being separated from them, I call to let their father know I would be at church. My mindset was on 'this is just a temporary setup.' I was happy and looking forward to coming back to church and seeing my children. He responded "well this Sunday is not good. Let us try next Sunday." I asked why. He made up some excuse and assured me kindly in his voice I could come to our church next Sunday. I sat there on the edge of the bed in disbelief and feeling desperate. I almost decided to go anyway, but I did not want to cause a scene in the church. Never in my life had anyone told me I could not attend a church, and he was not going to be a dictator on where I go worship. I was led to seek out a church to visit and pondered where to go. I remembered a church where my sister used to sing often, so I attend there. So, I took it upon myself to visit a new church for that Sunday with hopes of attending my church the following week. I genuinely enjoyed the service, and it gave me the strength I needed to carry me a little further. But I had to see my children. I longed to see and talk with them and to see that they were being cared for. Days and a week had gone by. It was becoming more and more unbearable because I could not hug and kiss their little faces or hear their laughter. Suppressing all my emotions each day with a scheduled six to eight-hour school week, study time, travel, and pretending to be copasetic among my peers was challenging.

Driving home from school one night, I felt lost and unwanted. This was becoming a reality of normalcy for me, which the adversary was trying to set up in my mind for me not to fight. There were far too many valuable pieces missing that were connected to my destiny, and their destiny connected to me. I had suppressed my emotions long enough. I could not wait to get into the house and go straight to my bedroom. I did not want to pull my car over as it was late and dark out. I ran up those wooden stairs. I could feel the submersion of tears that I was trying to hold back all day. The tears started flowing as I reached for the doorknob in my room. I could sense God's presence. As I closed the door, I felt as if God was greeting me. I felt helpless, full of hurt and pain that I had tried to suppress since my separation from my children... and then I completely broke down. I could not sniffle through the flood gates of tears that were bursting through like a dam. The tears had arrived, and I knew my Heavenly Father was there to comfort me. I had not turned on the lights and cried as my books were in my hands and my purse was on my shoulder; I just crumbled to the floor. I cried out to God loudly in prayer. I wailed loudly. I felt birthing pains like my children had been ripped away from my insides. "God help me," I asked. The pain was so unbearable. I did not deserve to be treated this way. I had not committed a transgression. I was faithful. A servant of God, a wife, and a loving mother. All I could do was give in to the pain and remain curled in a fetal position as I submerged myself into finding a solution, to find myself ... to be healed and gather my thoughts where I would not break under this mistreatment. I searched to find comfort. To hold on to myself and pray so I would not break, although I felt like I wanted to die because my children were wondering why I had not been home in a few weeks, I knew I could not give in. I saw no way out. All I could do was call on God. I was heartbroken. I had never endured this kind of cold-blooded pain that carried so much sadness. I missed my children so much.

A Step Ahead

Once I gained some barring in the days ahead, I contacted my spouse and told him I would be visiting the children. He was cruel in his response toward me, and instructed, "it would be best for the sake of the children that you not to come over; but if you do, to be sure to call first." What? This was a contradictive statement and odd because I had not heard that tone in his voice before. I meditate upon what had I done to deserve this estranged treatment. I was always faithful to him and never thought about cheating. I was always a loving parent. All marriages have their problems and differences, and since we were a Christian couple believing and living in the Word of God, I thought it

                                    Judah Moore

would be different. It should not have warranted that I looked like I was abandoning our children.

As a little time went by, I had a reality check while meditating on all that occurred within the past month with our marriage, the type of man my husband could have been if we were able to agree to disagree, and him taking on dutiful and fatherly responsibilities. Who and what would possess a married man to ask his wife to leave their three children requesting she leave the house? There was no consideration as to how our children would experience feelings of abandonment and insecurities. I had to realize I was no longer shielded, protected, or secure. I was on my own. A life I had lived as a caring mother did not matter to this "man of God." What an affront to the covenant of our marriage. In my baby steps as a born-again Christian, the first thing I learned was that God does things decently and in order, *"Let all things be done decently and in order." (I Corinthians 14:40, KJV)*; and in the unification of that, God designed marriages to be a relationship that represented human mankind and His relationship with us; and its spiritual components to submitting to one another. As a couple prays and asks God for direction throughout their marriage, He can take them through any storm … *"That he might present it to himself a glorious church, not having spot, or wrinkle, or any such thing: but that it should be holy without blemish" (Ephesians 5:27, KJV).* In the Book of Matthew, *"He saith unto them, Moses because of the hardness of your hearts suffered you to put away your wives: but from the beginning it was not so." (Matthew 19:8, KJV).*

My Tent, My Place of Refugee

I was still vesiculating back and forth with my brokenness, meaning *undergoing a change of positive essence of maturity.* God was operating on my spiritual growth by giving me more substance or "manna" from high to work in these difficult times. I thought about my children, and I know they wondered about their mother. But going into weeks my bouts of crying subsided bit by bit. My world seemed a tad clearer and less troublesome. Eventually, I knew their father would be contacting me because he was responsible for all our children's needs. I decided to focus on the environment and ambiance in my bedroom since I spent all my time secluded in my room. I visited some resale stores to create a comfortable sanctuary for prayer, meditation, and study. I wanted to bring all my outside pressures, concerns, and worries into my quiet space so that God could work on all my burdens as I brought them to His presence. This was my place to have quietness and peace. I dressed my bed with a white satin comforter and pillows along with a beige and white satin chaise lounge. I wanted to feel as if I was walking into my enclosed Egyptian tent-like sanctuary, a sacred place in all aspects. The dream I had inspired this décor. The vision which God had shown me, I was living it in technicolor. I believe as much as I wanted to spend time with God, that even He wanted to spend time with me, and I wanted to feel God's presence, His voice, and be at peace in a serene covering. There was even a small sunporch in the room for meditation, to feel a breeze or see and hear the birds singing beautiful melodies igniting the peace needed and filling my atmosphere with love. This would help me reflect on what would be coming my way. I had to grasp hold of this unexpected new life, which was forced onto me.

Judah Moore

After making these adjustments to my bedroom, I was feeling a bit stronger. Yet, just when I was able to see a glimmer of light and feel accomplished, and determine how to fine-tune my new lifestyle, there was a sudden knock at the backdoor of my sister's house. I wondered why and whoever it is knocking, how come they did not knock at the front door. There was no home but me. Both of my sisters were at work. I wondered who could be knocking on the back door of all places. As I walked through the kitchen and looked through the glass window, I saw there were three women from the church with who I spent much time in fellowship and prayer. So, by now I am wondering why now? Why and what is the point of this unexpected visit? How did they find out where I was living? I was quite hesitant about answering the door. Despite all that, I saw how happy they were to see me as I opened the door to let them in. I had been placed in an awkward position and did not fully know how or what to say. Really, I was not ready for anyone close to me to see me. I did not want to seem rude; therefore, it was hard to readily be open. I had to come to myself full circle and remember the good times we shared. I felt my heart leap for joy and that smile of mine returned to bless them with love. But it felt good to smile again and to be loved. I noticed they had bags in their hands. They each spoke and said, "We brought you food," and we laughed simultaneously. They had bags and bags of groceries and in return lots of hugs. Momentarily that dark cloud lifted off me, and I felt happy. I was extremely grateful to have these ladies in my life. I knew they appreciated our fond relationships. We filled the kitchen with laughter and chattered about how much we missed each other. I expressed how much I missed them and eventually sought out how much they knew about my living arrangement.

They were unaware of the full picture. I sensed that my spouse created a scenario for them to come to see about me because of his own guilt. So, I explained to them the reason I had not been attending our church. There was a strange quietness in the kitchen, and I could not help but feel that that strange presence was intentionally invited so she could return to give him full details about me. This lady was one I spent a lot of time counseling. She did not have the same kind of relationship that the other two had with me. But, that one lady knew more than all of us. After more conversation, my two prayer partners requested that we meet again for dinner at each other's house sometime soon. I hesitantly agreed to the idea but felt it would be good for me to be around those I knew so I could regain some normalcy in my life.

As I reflected and meditated more on the visit of my friends, I sensed that a seducing spirit had invaded my home where my children were living with their father. Why was I feeling particularly uncomfortable as we were all in the kitchen talking? And not only that, but its association was also always hiding in the background behind my lady friends, and even among other people in the church that I was close to. I was just remembering certain incidents. I believed that this person had embraced my counsel all the while envying what God had blessed me with yet finding ways to have alone time with my spouse while I was overseeing business. She was over at our house too much. In disbelief, I discovered it was apparent that my spouse had engaged in an emotional and physical affair at some point in our marriage and certainly with women in our church.

My evidence of inclinations did not prove me wrong. On a certain day unexpectantly, I went over to the house to

                                    Judah Moore

see my children. I was tired of the excuses made up by my children's father. I was fed up with him telling me why I needed to call first to get permission to see my children. It was late at night when I dropped by unannounced. In fact, it was after nine o'clock in the evening after I finished my class. The friend that came over to my sister's house answered the door. She greeted me kindly and I returned the same response. It was hard for me to ask any questions because I knew it would be a bad scene between us. She was dressed in bright-colored silk lounging pajama set. I looked at her and wondered what and why was she in my house, with my children. She swiftly asked me if I wanted to see my children, and I proceeded nicely moving toward the kitchen door from the breezeway without an answer. When I walked through the kitchen towards the bedrooms announcing myself, there was an unsettle in the atmosphere. We had two women who lived with us for many years, and I could tell they were extremely uncomfortable. My sons were sleeping, but my daughter was wide awake. Now, I was not going to go into a tirade about any of them, my only concerns were about the well-being of my children. I knew that she needed her mother's touch and her love. She stared at me with those pretty eyes. I wondered if she felt abandoned as I looked at her little pretty face. I touched her cheek giving her loving words and inspiration. I told her how much I loved her. And just comforted her little spirit the best I could without becoming too emotional. I saw her tears well up in her eyes, and I could tell she had strength like her mother. I promised that I would come back to get her, and her brothers. She shook her head, yes lying on her pillow with those bright eyes saying, "please." Their father was nowhere to be found. As I left the house without incident, I was overcome with emotion and feelings of helplessness. I wanted my children, but I had no place with ample room for us to stay.

The next time we had our didactic counseling course session, my assignment was to share with the group of eight students a stream of questions, to help resolve any issues or problems. This was a practice assignment on becoming experts in our counseling field of study. I was dreading this and talked to myself to keep it together. I did not want to share any of my personal business with this group, and with the therapist/instructor. The student who was playing the part of my therapist was a White woman who I admired because she genuinely loved all of us. She was like a married mature woman who had a large family, and she adopted all of us as her own. I was not sure how she would advise me on my current situation, but she began to filter through the process. As we sat directly across from each other, she asked a lot of open-end questions and I felt I could trust her and those listening. I was thinking to myself, 'ok this isn't that bad.' There was a response from her in which I reveal that I was no longer with the children's father and my children were living with him. I briefly explained how I missed my daughter without tearing up and I began to cry. The group was silent taking in what they heard. My instructor was shaken. I could tell by her stare. My classmate drew me back in and made me confront the ball of emotions I was feeling. I thought to myself, 'you mean there is more?' I thought I had dealt with most of it a few weeks ago, but she did not allow me to withdraw from the hurt, but to master it, to take control of it. Her knowledge of negotiation had given me the strength I needed to keep it all together and work through my situation realistically, I mean really. At the end of our counseling session, she closed with words of her understanding about how I felt concerning my missing my

                                        Judah Moore

children giving me words of comfort. As we went through our master's program, she made sure to check on me and made sure I was okay, always giving me inspiration and words of encouragement. I appreciated her thoughtfulness. However, as I expected word with my classmates knew my dilemma, and she wanted to pry more into the decision-making made by the children's father. I could not go inside my ex's head to determine why he said what he said. As far as I was concern, it was said, and it was done. I did not want to spend my time any further on it and decided to close myself off from communicating with anyone concerning my situation. What was more important for me was graduating from seminary so that I could find a place for me and my children to live. And somehow, I knew God would work everything out as I moved onward in this wilderness experience of deserted land.

Now before being isolated from my home, I unknowingly discovered that I was being disconnected from the church as well. My weekly Sunday morning conversations with my children's father (where he felt it was best that I did not visit the church on Sunday which he kept promising I could return soon) turned out to be untrue. I called to ask whether I could come back to our church after seeing my daughter, and it was always the same answer, "not this Sunday." So, what was I supposed to do? Go into our church and make my presence known, walking up into the pulpit, and making an announcement of how deceitful their pastor had been in our marriage and risking a scene in front of my children scarring them for life? Or being on all the News channels for causing a raucous and subsequently being escorted out the doors of the church? I had seen this happen once before by another member when I was pastoring with him. It was humiliating and she did not deserve that type of treatment. However, my not being able to return to my church did not stop me from fellowshipping elsewhere to hear the gospel preached.

In Search for the Spirit of God

At this moment, I had to shift my thinking into a different role in my life, which was being solely independent. I believed God would be giving me a new passage into history to share my trials, tribulations, and victories. In retrospect, it was not easy. But I was eager to find myself, to be true to myself, and to others, whomever God put in my path. It was tough functioning through the deep-rooted bitterness and anger I had toward my children's father at times. This was a battleground I had to overcome. The enemy wanted to take hold of my mind, to hold it hostage, and enchain me into a dark deep depression; but I refused to allow the enemy to win. I was not giving up on my relationship with God, no matter how I felt. I knew I had to keep my prayer life alive for my edification. I had to pour my essence of love and goodness into my children. For I know it was just as awkward for them. It was not about how I felt … they gave me meaning and purpose to fight and to live on.

I visited a second church, and by this time I was feeling that I needed and wanted more than just a brief relationship or encounter with a church. I wanted to belong and to be accepted in a church that involved all my imperfections, my baggage, and hurt, all without judgment; but to be cared for, understood, and given godly wisdom. I know there is no perfect church, but I so desired that perfect church for me. I did not enjoy church hopping, never did. My relationship with God was much more than spending time in a church and being unfulfilled. So, I went to my

                                    Judah Moore

heavenly Father and prayed. I asked God to direct me to a church where I could grow spiritually. I was not interested in being a minister in any sort of role. I needed to be ministered to. I wanted to be healed from the pain and emotional suffering caused by this separation. I took it further and asked God that whomever the preacher (male or female) would be that they spoke the truth, rightly dividing the Word of Truth and not compromising the content of the Bible by leaning to their understanding. My prayers were thought out with specifics as they should be because I feared God, and I did not ever want to leave the church if I had another encounter as I did with my children's father who used the Word of God for his glorification. I would be lost without my Savior, and I knew that that devil wanted to pull me back into the world after losing everything.

From childhood, I participated in the church as I mentioned before, but my involvements were short-lived in attendance because they had moved. Growing up as I entered my early teen years, I ventured into visiting several churches of various denominations in our demographic area trying to find a church like the one I was attending. Finally, after I found a church that I enjoyed attending, I was baptized at 13 in a Baptist church but strayed away from church altogether when I entered high school. My home life did not warrant normalcy, and as a result, I became a seeker of love and acceptance finding no one who could feel the voids in my life. It is so amazing how God works in our lives because it was not until I met my children's father that I returned to the church. I do believe it was an appointed time in my life. I grew steady and fast once I recommitted my life and walk with God. I was in search of whatever God had for me. As our church grew, God sent respectable and virtuous teachers and prophetess who spent time with me teaching and ministering to my thirst and boldness to want to know more about the spiritual gifts and callings. Our relationships were seasonal. But as Apostle Paul writes to the church, *"I have planted, Apollos watered; but God gave the increase. So then neither is he that planteth anything, neither he that watereth; but God that giveth the increase." (I Corinthians 3:6-7, KJV).* And I gladly received the increase of God's wisdom and worked at being an imitator of Christ… *"Be ye therefore followers of God, as dear children; And walk in love, as Christ also hath loved us, and hath given himself for us an offering and a sacrifice to God for a sweet-smelling savour." (Ephesians 5:1-2, KJV),* until I did not see that old creation, but the new creation that God wanted me to possess from my day of inception. *"Therefore, if any man be in Christ, he is a new creature: old things are passed away; behold, all things are become new." (II Corinthians 5:17, KJV).*

Throughout our ministry together, I could see God blessing us as we worked together in His vineyard; planting, watering, and blossoming saints to do God's perfect will. We repeated our wedding vows for our eighth anniversary. Our children were 6, 3, and 1 year of age. Our family tie was strong. We were building a committed relationship with one another. And, to the ministerial work which we were given charge to watch and pray over. It was also our church anniversary. What a way to celebrate what God had put together. But as we grew through the years, more temptation and disagreements entered our relationship. There was never an agreement at the end of our disagreements, except on Sundays when we were both involved in our tasks and ministerial responsibilities. We began to lose members here and there. But before they would leave, they came to me with apologies stating they could no longer attend our

Judah Moore

church. They wanted to stay but felt the preaching and conduct by the pastor were not lining up with the Word of God. I was heartbroken when our members would leave because I recognized they were faithful. They made it clear to me that the messages that were being preached by him were different. As a result, we lost more good laborers from the church who I felt were sent to do extensive outreach and help add a culture of worship and thanksgiving to the church. Despite this though, our church was still growing. People were starting to come from everywhere. We were close to the two-hundred mark after thirteen years of church growth. God was using me more in the pulpit. I was fellowshipping with other pastor wives, and it was refreshing. For these reasons in my prayer to God, I told Him I was not interested in preaching in this state of mind whenever he sent me to another church. I wanted to start over and be a student. Yes, to start over again. How could I minister to anyone with brokenness and bitterness in my heart over a man who misrepresented the Word of God without blame? During this era, several pastor wives were getting divorced. However, they were starting their own churches and moving on productively. Nonetheless, this was the last thing I wanted. I just could not spew my shattered heart of resentment into someone else's life. I had to find myself first. I had to love myself. I needed to be totally healed, not partly healed, and not faking it until I make it healed! But stripped, remolded, shaped, carved, and put on the shelf until I became a pure vessel for Jesus my Savior. I wanted to learn, to be taught, and to give Jesus all of me.

God's Visit in A Dream

As I slept one night, God came to me in a dream, and in that dream, I was approaching a huge church. It had large columns one on each side of its corners. I remember feeling excited in my dream about entering the church as I approached the first stairstep. It was a massive building. The chambered doors were shut. I could see the antiqueness of the brass handles on the two doors, which would both swing open together. I was looking up at the building, and as I began to take my first step to go up the marble stairs, suddenly the chamber doors swung open, and there poured out dozens of women who were all moving in like a slow-motion movie … they were dressed in assorted designs of black and white. They had distinct designs and patterns which were long wedding dresses. The dresses were flowing or swaying in the air so carefree as they ran out of the church in slow motion. Some women had the color pattern of a black eye mask on their faces with all white dresses. Some had more of the black color mixed with white, without an eye mask and some had the color black more than others. I looked in amazement and wondered as I stood and stared at them why were their wedding gowns covered with puzzle-type shapes of black and white. One thing I noticed, these women were happy, as if they had been let loose and they welcomed their freedom at last. I looked to see further if there was anyone in the overflow of women I recognized. The crowd started to dwindle, and in the final moment, I recognized my mother was in the crowd of women. Unbelievable! My mother did not look my way as she passed by me, but neither did the others. I pondered and waited for God to reveal the interpretation of the dream to me. Well, a few days passed, and I entered another dream.

God had shown me getting out of my car and walking toward a large white stone-like church. I could not see the front of it because I had a distance to reach the front of the building. This was the end of my second dream. Sometimes

God will show us in part or give us a glimpse, and not a conclusion to the vision. I suppose the Lord wanted me to focus on every detail of that dream to understand the depths of the interpretation which He wanted me to know. The next sequential from the second dream as He revealed to me later in the third part, is that I was walking up against the wall of this large stone-like building. I remember walking and looking down at the same time because the sidewalk was not fully expansive in width, just enough to walk straight. I was conscious of the cracks in the pavement and did not want to fall. As I got closer to the front of the building, there comes a man dressed in all-black apparel with a large camera on his back. He was persistent in capturing me on camera, as I was trying to shy away. I was getting close to the front of the building, and as I got closer to the end of my path, I looked up and saw a large column. I thought, in my dream finally, I am going to see more of this huge building. I was full of expectations. As I approached closer in full view of the column, I looked up and saw words inscribed on the column, but the camera operator kept distracting me. I could not make out what the words were, but when I woke up, I thought that the camera man sure made an impressible statement for me, "in that whatever we are given to do, make sure you do it to its fullest extent." Although I was not able to make out the name of the building in my dream, in the days ahead I was at peace. I was confident God would show me, tell me, and reveal what He wanted to impart in my spirit, as it would be for my good and my purpose to continue to exist in trusting only Him.

CHAPTER TWO

"And Being ..."

~~~

Some weeks had gone by. I chose to stand still in the crystal sands beneath my feet and wait to hear the voice of God's whisper leading me to my destination of the joy of no more pain and shame. I thought often about the dream God had given to me. I had no further interest in just visiting churches. I desired to be at the one God desired for me to be present. I hungered and thirsted for so much more. I wanted to dismiss any feelings of abandonment and embarrassment initiated by my soon-to-be ex-spouse. By this time, he filed for divorce. I had even communicated with him about staying together for the sake of our children until they graduated from high school. It seems throughout my developmental years as a child, I always experienced some form of abandonment. Yet God was here now, not that He ever was not present, but I knew I had Him all to myself and I was not alone in my journey. Fully present. With no distractions. I was recognizing in parts that He wanted my total attention and being, but more in a larger capacity. He was my total reason for not giving up. Thus, I was on a mission. A mission to regain full possession to hold my children again in my arms. Despite the spiritual battles ahead, I knew I would find myself, my soul, and learning to love my innermost being of who I am.
~~~

Breakthrough of Final Dream

I was relaxing at home one Sunday afternoon watching television. I had stopped the urge of trying to fulfill a void in my life by wanting to visit other churches. I was sitting in a patio-like room apart from my sister's living room. It is funny because after being in her house for almost two months, I had not ventured into this quaint space in her house as I turned on the television. I was scanning this intimate room that was full of her plant arrangements complemented by vintage-type windows which blazed warm sunlight within this cozy area. Suddenly, my attention was drawn away and captured by a commercial on the television set. It was about a church service. I remembered my prayer request, and I was all ears. I was immediately drawn to the sound and voice of the commercial and have thus far enjoyed what I heard. I had taken my eyes off the screen for a minute, and it had shown part of the church, but I was able to get a quick glance and the commercial advertisement of the church started to look very familiar. I watched and was glued with discernment as to whether this church place would be a good attend. I continued to watch in full anticipation sensing my spirit stirring with excitement. In closing the advertisement, quickly showed the structure of the building, the color, and the pillars. I was waiting for the name; the location; and the time in which their services began. The location of the church was in full view now. I was stunned, shocked, and full of amazement because this was the church that I had dreamt about. The statuesque large, majestic stone building was surely the place God had shown me in my dream. Oh, my goodness I thought to myself. I could feel the tears wail up in my eyes because God had answered my prayers. I had memorized the service time and was extremely grateful that God was leading me to

His place where I could find Him and be part of a body that worshipped the Lord in Spirit and in Truth.

What made it even better was that the church was in my old neighborhood where I grew up. I had played in this same building when I was in junior high, running up and down the slanted ramps with my friends when it was vacant; and on another occasion when I had my graduation ceremony from high school. I was flabbergasted with disbelief and wonderment. But I was awe-stricken by God's faithfulness and thoughts toward me. I never imagined in a million years He would lead me back to a familiar place. I sat and sat reflecting on my life transformations. I was following the plan of God. I could not figure it all out, but it was not meant for me to figure it out! Just go, I thought! I was so happy and excited. I had made up my mind that coming Sunday, I would be present at a new church.

My Sunday Church Visit

I woke up early to arrive on time for church service that Sunday morning in November. I was walking on a new path. I was leaving behind the possibility of ever going back to my church home and having to ask permission to return. God had now given me another door to walk through, and I was full of expectation.

I pulled up in the parking lot and was directed to park my car. I walked the same steps that were shown to me in my dream. As I walked alongside the brick wall and watched my steps on the pavement, I reached the first column before turning the corner and stepping onto a sheet of marble flowing toward the entrance doors, as it opened with God's precious angels greeting me with open arms and a warm welcome. I immediately felt the presence of the

Holy Spirit breathe on me at the entrance as I walked in and relaxed as I was taking in all the beauty that radiated in the lobby … and straightway humbling to be submissive and obedient to the power of God's presence. As my footsteps walked to the sanctuary doors, I remember reflecting on the years gone by as a youth. I passed by people in the lobby who were busy with their assignments as I made my way toward the entry doors to go into the sanctuary. I could smell a beautiful aroma of the presence of God that would make a person have a humble posture as I could still feel the presence of God even more. I was filled with hope and expectation.

I intentionally arrived at the church rather early for my own personal observations. I wanted to see what God had gifted me with. As I walked into the sanctuary, I noticed a few people present. I stopped in my tracks as I thought about where to sit, and then I had a thought about someone seeing me. I had not considered these concerns before leaving home that I would personally have for myself. This was bad. This had become a serious dilemma as to run into someone that knew me. And that thought had just crossed my mind. I was saying to myself, "Lord, please don't let me run into anyone that knows me." I found myself being preoccupied with this thought way too much. I wanted to focus on just being present, and nothing else. I knew if I did run into someone who knew me, they would be quite surprised that I was visiting a different church and would want to know why. I purposely selected a spot in the middle of the massive sanctuary, hoping once the seats started to fill in, that I would blend in. I needed to re-focus my thoughts and get settled. I began to gaze upon the interior and design of the stunning sanctuary. I was admiring the modern architecture, elegant style, and colors that blended impeccably. The inside looked so different from what I had remembered before. I sat meditating and gathering my thoughts and breathing in the liberation of freedom I had which was fueling my sadness with joy. I suddenly noticed the familiar face of one of our old church members. She was one of our older members during our fourth year in ministry when my oldest was an infant. She operated in the gifts of healing and prophecy. Often, I attended several of her women's events in the past which were very inspiring. But I prayed that she did not notice me. I was watching her. She was casually getting herself organized and then she began to nonchalantly walk in my direction. At this point, she was not really paying attention to her surroundings. "Oh, my goodness," I thought … "she is going to be coming my way." I was watching her closely. She walked past the pulpit area and turned up the aisle toward me. Once our eyes locked, her facial expression was of shock. She walked toward and over to me. She said with a high-pitched voice, "Pastor, what are you doing here?" I know how it looked! 'Out of place.' I hesitated in responding to her. I did not want to divulge my personal issue or situation. Up to this point, I was feeling simply fine … but that heartache returned in being separated from my children and being asked to leave my home all started to resurface coming to remind me of my reality. She looked at me and saw my eyes wailing up in tears, as I tried to find words of justification. She stopped being inquisitive. She stopped asking questions. I just could not find the words for all her answers. I knew she understood. She was a seasoned evangelist now, full of boldness and the gift of discernment that she carried since our first meet. She laid hands on my shoulders to put me at ease and calm my spirit. (I surely did not want to have to go to the lady's room to try to get myself together). I was

                                                          Judah Moore

relieved she gave me the comfort I needed to keep my composure. She went on to say, "it is well Pastor. You can fellowship here with us as long as you need to." I was trying hard to hold back my flood of tears, as I nodded and told her thank you with a smile.

Well, after my encounter with my dear sister in Christ, I saw things were starting to come together for the morning worship service. The intercessors in the church all came together, the elders and their wives and others postured themselves at the alter and began to pray for the move of the Holy Spirit of God. The camera ministry was poising themselves for service and I spotted the camera operator I saw in my dreams. I said to myself, "Oh, my goodness Lord, that's the man you showed me in my dream." I smiled and thanked God for His awesomeness in how He showed me in the dream every point of corporeality. The organist played ministering music which helped to soothe my soul. I could feel God's presence in the church. I was so grateful to be amongst other Christians who were loving laborers and sincere while they prepared the atmosphere for worship. I could only imagine how their praise and worship would be, as I thought to myself. My expectation was waiting and wanting all God had for me on this day. I knew I was ready to sit at Jesus' feet to gain clarity in my life. I was ready to partake in the blessing that my Heavenly Father had stored up for me to become and be all He wanted me to become.

Entering Worship

The instruments began to play, and the music flowed throughout the church. We entered worship all on one accord. The voices of angels began to praise our glorious Lord; my soul and my spirit awaken to the breath of God. I tried to hold onto all the mixed emotions from missing my children to be separated from my church, but I could not hold onto my tears of sadness, but it was a joy to experience God's love. I sensed I was walking into a realm of worship at its highest level of purity. I had never experienced such a beautiful time in a worship service. I was being washed, cleansed, and healed as we sang throughout the service. As the pastor came forward, I heard the thunders of God come from his voice. His articulation was concise and full of power as he dove into the interpretation of God's word inspiring the hearts of the congregation of believers and non-believers. I am sure they were touched. I listened intently amongst the crowd and was amazedly astonished by the illumination in how the Word of God was being delivered. The presentation of ministry and articulating the Word of God was very opposite to what I was associated with my children's father. I longed for this kind of teaching again which I received as a child in my very first church. My spirit leaped with joy. This is what I needed. Truth! The teachings met me where I was in my spiritual walk and confirmed the knowledge I gained as a Christian throughout my studies and ministering. I realize the enemy's plan was to take away God's gift from me which 'it' had attempted to do so many times before, and that was to try and take away my state of mind. Isn't this the first thing the enemy wants to take from us so that we can totally miss God's purpose for our life? There were no divisional rants being preached on this day. The truth was being taught here. There were no made-up reasons or excuses as to why a person/people should not be obedient. There was no self-exaltation or glorification, demeaning or judging people in the congregation. Today there were meaningful intentions to deliver an all-inspiring message of God's goodness and

                                          Judah Moore

grace. I could feel my soul and spirit settle because I heard the TRUTH on this day. Hallelujah!

I walked away after church feeling relieved and so hopeful. God used His vessel to preach a much-needed word for me. All I wanted was to feel God's presence, and I did. All I wanted was to lay my burdens on the altar, and my heart did that in worshipping Him. Only God knew what I was suffering. And I praised Him with all I had because I wanted Him to know how much I needed Him in this mess of deceitfulness. All I wanted was to know that God had not forgotten about me, and He had not. As I faced the battles of being absent from my children, I had been divinely fueled and ready to take on my challenges for the week to come.

Boldness

I continued faithfully going to my new church. No one could move or interfere with where I was fellowshipping and worshipping. This was a sealed covenant between me and God. I was still in phases of adjusting to the fresh changes in my life. I had to travel every other week for school, study, and look for work. Not only that, here I was, still a married woman without an accountable husband, a man who no longer wanted to remain married, who had our children, and who wanted to order me to call first before coming to see them. With my being present in the church and hearing the word, I was gaining more strength, clarity, and boldness in dealing with this abnormal circumstance. I never recall any man of God doing this to their wife. What was the matter with him? There may be some or many women in this predicament who would have overseen this situation differently. Yet all battles are different. I did not want to shake the fragmented foundation of not having my children in my life. I had to trust that my children were being cared for properly as my schedule was etched out for another four months. It was important that I completed school in my last semester. I was not going to quit as I was so close to completion. When I lived at the home, we had two elder women who lived with us. One of the sisters collaborated closely with me to ensure my children had what they needed. And they were still living there in my absence, so I was a bit relaxed with them being there to help with their everyday tasks. This was never my idea to have anyone live with us long-term in a span of ten years, ever. But with our church schedule of managing two churches, the children's father thought this would be perfect for our household to run more smoothly.

Seeing Clearly

Reflecting on this time past, I had a keen suspicion of someone else working their way in or who had already worked their weight in being around my children and their father. Subsequently, I was unequipped to fight this battle strategically, as I was trying to figure out my own direction and emotionally survive through this turmoil. These sacks of bags were heavy and filled with impositions, abandonment, shame, isolation, mistreatment, and all the other tentacles attached to it were hindering me to pursue any progress which I would normally be able to master. Distractions are where the enemy wants us to be. Now God was my clear focus across the oasis of my journey. I had been blinded by this life decision. God could see for me, and if I prayed for direction in the purest sense intense to audibly hear His voice, then I knew the power of the Holy Spirit would move with me. In all, I was in search of peace so I could hear clearly from God. I needed God's strength to have the ability to tackle this dysfunctional decision of removing and separating a mother from her children.

A Pastor's Wife Prayer: Lord Arrest Me

Yet there was an added separation in my life I had to confront. The pastor had his lovely wife come to the pulpit to pray over our offerings and tithes on Sunday. I had never heard her pray before. She began to intercede for us as she entered the depths of her secret prayer closet. The move of God pours out of her and within the holy place as she began to cry out, "Lord, arrest me," with her hands behind her back. Within her prayer, she continued to repeat these words. The Spirit of God touched me so deeply and took me beyond my present situation onto another part of my life that I needed to confront. She continued to pray and minister to us on these two words which stood out plainly, Lord "arrest me," she said fervently. There was a thick and heavy presence of God in the church that hour, and I had visualized a bright white cloud facing her straightway from heaven with all His Glory beaming with gladness hearing her bearing her submissive heart, commitment, and love for Christ. My God I thought to myself. What a powerful woman of God. Somewhere in her expression I was completely convicted, (*Merritt, 1997*). Then Lord began to speak to me and told me I needed to surrender myself and go to my parent's home and speak with them.

Well, I knew this was not going to be an easy assignment for me because my parents and I had not communicated in years, mainly because of my children's father. He was not fair to my mother, nor to my extended family members which were why my mother left the church. At one time my close relatives, a couple of my sisters, and my parents were all a part of our ministry, and then suddenly one Sunday and thereafter, they never returned giving no explanation. No one in my family ever reached out to me and over the years I had developed animosity toward them. So, after a wonderful service, I headed over to my parent's house to start removing this wedge between us.

My parents lived about ten minutes away from the church. While driving to the house that I grew up in, I began reflecting on the changes in my life. I had so much compassion and good memories as I reflected, and furthermore that God in His infinite wisdom was bringing me right back where it started. I had an unfinished life journey that needed to be reconciled. To paraphrase, one author writes, *"There comes a time in our relationship with God and our walk with Christ when we must allow the Holy Spirit to place us under Spiritual Arrest. It is not a pleasant sensation"* (Lyons, 2017, para. 1). These were reasons why my life was being scattered in working my way toward the path God wanted me to walk in. Honestly, how can one be a testimony carrying the same weathered baggage? God wants to discard our old ways and life, so we can glorify Him through our deliverance of testimonies. I was the one being arrested by myself, and it was for my good so that God could use me with a pure heart. I needed to confront the unforgiveness which I held onto since my childhood which helped create an almost permanent detachment. I realized when you are going through your own personal issues in life, there will be a more important part to oversee which will give more clarity to your entire situation. Thy Kingdom Come Ministry, Inc. denotes, *"God will not place you under Spiritual Arrest. It is an Arrest that must be willingly submitted to. It is, however, still conducted under the spiritual authority of the Holy Spirit. The next thing about being placed under arrest is that you lose your freedom,"*

Judah Moore

(*Lyons, 2017, para. 2*). God cared about my situation, but He wanted me to capture the entire picture. He wanted me connected to my lifelines as they would catapult my purposes. God does not want to hear of our excuses and ramblings of what He already knows when we come before His presence. In this case, God wanted me to confront being uncomfortable for a greater work. And as I was driving, I was thinking about how life had changed me greatly since I left home. But in a sense, I felt like I was losing a part of the ole me. I needed my mother, and I hoped she felt the same. But at this point, I did not want to be questioned about my marriage. Or hear, "I told you so." I just wanted to 'be.' When my parents got on one accord, they were a dynamic duo and very outspoken, and today, I did not want this as it would run me away. I needed to be understood, not agitated, just loved. I needed them to listen without judgment. I just needed to feel at home once again.

Visiting my Parents

Here I am, parking and getting out of my car, stepping onto the sidewalk where my name was etched before the cement was hardened way back in the day. It reminded me of the scripture, *"When I was a child, I spake as a child, I understood as a child, I thought as a child: but when I became a (wo)man, I put away childish things." (1 Corinthians 13:11, KJV)*. But, although the scripture speaks volumes about my developmental character, I could not seem to rise above that feeling of being a child. One stairstep at a time I walked up and braced myself before knocking on the door. I reflected on my present image as a woman preacher standing on the porch dressed in my church suit and heels looking over the neighborhood and how much it had changed over the years. I never thought of being a pastor's wife when growing up. I felt God had called me to be a healer when I was a child, yet I never imagined having so much passion and responsibility for people. After completing my walk up those familiar stairsteps onto the porch, I could not help but reflect on how I and my neighborhood friends used to play Jacks. Our street was so full of happy kids riding on bikes, playing those Motown sounds, roller-skating, walking to the corner store, and even yelling good morning to one another from across the street or waving down the street, but now the street was much quieter and isolated.

My lifespan of entering and exiting throughout my evolving years was quite expansive as I reflected upon the years. My heart was beating fast before I knocked on the door as I was taking in the uncomfortableness of going back into some sour memories, yet playful and fun memories when the time of village communities was influential. I knocked on the door and patiently waited. I knocked again, but a little harder. My mom finally came to the door. She looked at me with shock and her mouth partially opened maintaining her maternal ground. She said, "Oh what are you doing here?" I said briefly, "I just came from church and wanted to come by for a few to see how she and dad were doing." I could tell she was caught off guard and more surprised than anything. She let me into the house, and I gave her a kiss. I could feel her awkwardness, so I immediately asked if dad was home. I did this so she could gather herself and gain composer. She pointed toward the back and sat in her chair as I went directly to him and said, "Hey dad," and gave him a hug. He was incredibly surprised to see me and asked where I was coming from. I replied with glee, "church." Being the dad who raised me, he asked "what church?" This left me giving him a brief synopsis of

                                                Judah Moore

everything that happened, and after I told him, he sat speechlessly. I immediately headed back toward the living room with my mother trying to avoid the millions of questions that were coming from him. I was not ready to discuss significant details with him. As I sat across from my mother, all we did was stare at each other. She did not know what to say. I did not know where to start. There was so much hurt and pain between the two of us. I needed to allow some space on my visits until we were naturally able to communicate with each other. I wanted her to heal as well as myself. Just knowing that my mom was still in my life was a blessing to me. So thereafter, every Sunday after church, I headed over to my parent's house. My normal stopover routine was just sitting and briefly visiting. My visits became longer and longer still with complete quietness, watching television or sitting on the porch. These times of visiting gave me time to heal, reflect, and speak to some old friends in the neighborhood. I was sure God was working with my mother too. I noticed one day my mom began to look at my physical appearance. She was a fashionista when we were younger attending church. I always tried wearing her expensive shoes. She was so pretty. Our mother always made sure we were adorned nicely, whether in play clothes or church clothes. But although I dressed like a lady, I was broken on the inside. I sensed I reminded her of how she dressed so sharply when she was going to church with all her daughters. I proudly mimicked her style and loved everything she wore. Yet it had been weeks, and we were not communicating, just sitting in the same room with brief chit-chats.

I was determined to remain still no matter how long I felt uncomfortable. I was not going to stop visiting. The founder of Thy Come Ministries denotes, *"for God to reach a conclusion in some areas, He must perform in and through our spirits. He must "detain, hold, or arrest" us for a while. That being our mobility, our freedom, our movement, must be spiritually restricted. As mentioned, this is not a pleasant experience, but it is a necessary one for the fullness of development for which God has ordained for our lives. We must accept the challenge of being placed in spiritual detention,"* (Lyons, 2017, para. 3). I needed my mom; and surely as time went on, we carefully began to mend our communication bit by bit; length by length into an entire way of communicating normally. It took several months for this to occur. She began to share with me the hurts she experienced, and why our other relatives left our church. She said emphatically, "I didn't say anything because I wanted you to know for yourself what kind of man you were married to!" I could not fault her for that, because if she had told me then, at the time, I cannot say how I would have dealt with it. Nevertheless, had I known; I could have prayed about it, and then put all my ducks in a row, I believe I would have been in a better predicament overall.

I began to reflect on what my mother discussed with me. I felt so far from my children. Their absence was starting to wear on me. I recalled a time when my stepfather was attending our Sunday services regularly by himself after my relatives left, and eventually, he stopped attending. He really enjoyed being with his grandchildren and the people in the church loved him. He had a very charismatic personality and was a sharp dresser too. He had even given his life to Christ one summer day one-year before my departure from the church when I ministered. I had ministered more than normal during this time and when my stepfather came to the altar in the middle of my message, I was stunned. I came down and immediately stood before him, and he said, "I want to give my life over to Christ." I proceeded to pray with him and introduce him to His Savior as he spoke the confessions of the death, burial, and resurrection of Christ from his heart. So, when I visited my parents after leaving the church that next Sunday, I had a talk with my dad. I asked him if he could do me a favor. He was all ears. I proceeded to ask, "dad would you go back to the church for me and keep an eye on the children?" I knew if I went through those doors of the church that it would be an ugly scene because the children's father was not being honest to the members, and plus I would never want to cause a disturbance in a church. But with my dad's wit of brassiness and boldness, I knew that the children's father would not say anything negative about me while he was present. He said, "Sure, I'll be glad to go and keep an eye on them." So, each Sunday thereafter I left my new church to visit my parents. My dad would share and talk about my children's behavior and anything else that was pertinent to their well-being. I felt so much better that I had my father present in their lives, whom I always looked to as my father, using his paternal authority and concern to watch over his grandchildren.

Gaining Momentums

The new year was here, and I made the decision to join my new church home. This was a huge step for me in my life. My children's father had already finalized our marriage and began the divorce proceedings without my knowledge. I was a single Christian mother of three children by March 1997. However, his decision had nothing to do with my spiritual relationship and where God was leading me. I was not going to step away from God due to his own selfish decision. My God had already set me up to be blessed with fresh manna, and I was going to glean from it until I was fully equipped and stuffed with what God wanted for me. I had no desire in looking back. I just wanted my children. My thoughts were consumed with gathering up my children, and the mere deliberations of what God had in store for them excited me. I wanted each of my children to experience a new fulfilled life with their mother, and where I had planted myself to grow spiritually, and healthier under the power and authority of faithful spiritual leaders.

Spring was nearing my graduation. Somehow to my surprise, I was missing a total of eight credits. I met with my advisor, who was concerned that I would not be able to graduate on time. He revealed carrying eighteen credits would be too difficult for me to attain. My own understanding could not agree to settle for graduation later. I only had a few months to complete my writing assignments and to complete my internship. My mind was made up and my confessions were "No, this will not be happening later. I will be graduating in a few months." I meditated hard on this and began to pray to ask for God's direction. He gave me a strict blueprint to follow to complete my writings. I grabbed the vision. I began to write out my plan, my steps, and dates to determine when I could spend time writing my papers while completing my internship as a Chaplain. God reminded me that I did not need to have any distractions, and He was with me every step of the way. I had no outside influences enter my plans which meant that I rarely communicated with my children during this time. I knew the outcome would be greater than my present regarding giving them all my undivided attention. I was on a mission. I was determined to prove to my advisor and myself that I would be graduating in May. The church was my strength. I wanted to *"And he shall be like a tree planted by the rivers of water,*

                                        Judah Moore

that bringeth forth his fruit in his season; his leaf also shall not wither; and whatsoever he doeth shall prosper." (Psalm 1:3, KJV). I had no plans of missing what the Word of God had for me, and all else that would be shared to enlighten and inspire me to move forward into the next level of our life.

As the time came closer to my graduation, I announced to my sister that I would be moving soon. It was unusual for me to make a statement like this because I normally plan out how I will be doing things. I just believed in my heart that I would be moving, and it would be happening soon. I had faith. As I was finishing completing my coursework assignments and preparing for graduation, my ex-husband contacted me with regards to my living situation. I briefly mentioned that I had explored a certain apartment available for move-in. At this point, I was trying to figure out how I was going to get the money I needed to fulfill the whole payment. He called me back in a day or so and asked where I wanted to live. I gave him the information, and to my surprise, he asked and encouraged me to investigate vacancies and pricing as soon as I could. When we spoke again, I gave him all the details. He shared that he would be able to provide everything, and I let him know I wanted our children to live with me. Once that was said, he assisted in making sure we had a place to live at the location I specified and where I always wanted to live even when we were married. Some weeks had gone by before my move-in date which was a few weeks before my graduation. My dear Uncle to my deceased biological father had even helped in making sure I had everything I needed to move us all in. Once things were finalized, I started the process of enrolling my children in their respective school's way in advance before they came to live with me. I was still drafting papers but almost finished. I had no beds, sofa, or tables, not even dishes. I had not fully figured out how I was going to take care of my three children alone at this point, but I was excited that they were coming to live with me. I was so focused on completing school, that this had just dawned on me, yet I still trusted God to provide for us.

God's Precious Gifts

I completed all my coursework and was able to graduate on time. In the meantime, their father brought our children over to their new two-bedroom, two-bathroom apartment. I was so happy. My children came into the apartment with their belongings and walked through the door finding me standing there to greet and hug them. They were looking stunned and amazed at their pristine environment and so happy to see me. I continually hugged them and encouraged them to walk around freely to view the place while I briefly communicated with their father. I was still upset with him for choosing not to work on our marriage for the sake of our children at least until they graduated from high school. When I discussed this with him some months earlier while living with my sister, he was so adamant about hearing from the Lord telling him that "I was not his wife." This thought had to leave my mind quickly. I thanked him and closed the door …and it was us, just us looking at each other. Their big bright eyes stared at me with love and expectation. I stood looking happily for us and visualizing the plans I had for their lives; not knowing that everything would not be perfect for us. (Meaning that in the years to come, we would experience financial hardships, health issues, eviction, return to live with their father, depression, and my return to homelessness due to job losses). But at present, the one vital goal I had for my children was to show them the pure love of God, and how to trust Him with all

                                    Judah Moore

their hearts, mind, and soul. I could not wait to introduce them to my new church. I knew they would love being there as I did. They had no idea that I was going to a different church. Our times together had been few when I lived with my sister. As much as I wanted to talk with them, I wanted to avoid them asking when I will be returning home; or where I was, etc. My intentions were to keep their hearts and minds undisturbed and peaceful. I wanted to avoid any acting out behaviors because of sadness or any other ugly or negative energy that wanted to latch on to them. In my prayer closet and worship, it was my intercession to specifically pray and asked God to watch over them and keep them safe. It had been exactly eight months of my being without my children. They missed a lot of nurturing and love that only a mother could give. Now, I had them in my arms, in my possession near and around me. I was now able to breathe. I was so gratefully thankful in my heart for God keeping them safe and secure in His arm.

Graduation Day

We had to get up early the next morning for the graduation. I had packed their clothes to change in on our travels to Ohio. I had driven to Ashland, Ohio so many times by myself or commuted with my classmates for our classes that I had our timing and arrival spot on. So, we stopped at one of my favorite restaurants halfway there and changed all their clothes, which left us at least another half hour to arrive at the church where the graduation was to be held. I was rushing at this point. When we arrived, everyone was helping each other with their caps and gowns. When my classmates, who were in my didactic counseling practicum saw me with my children who I spoke about during our times in class, they immediately asked their family members who were present to take my children under their wings, and they gladly obliged. I was running behind, and they all helped me with my cap and gown. The church was packed. I was proud to share this monumental time with my children. I wanted this to be a stamp of remembrance with my children for their accomplishment in holding while their mother was absent in their lives and empowering them to see the benefits of not quitting or giving up on what they believe in.

On our way back home, we celebrated with ice cream at a Dairy Queen off the road. The fresh air did us good, especially for me because my eyelids were getting heavy. My oldest son full of wisdom just kept talking to me asking me a million and one questions because he saw I was getting sleepy while driving. As I came to attention, I noticed for the first time that my oldest son had a unique quality of intuition that I had not had the chance to observe before. I looked into my rearview mirror reflecting on a Kodak moment watching my children enjoying the taste and pleasantries of ice cream and their freedom, and it did my heart good as we drove into the sunset enjoying the breeze from a long hot summer day. When we arrived at our new home, our new apartment, we all collapsed on our floor pallets side by side sleeping in the arms of God.

While I did not have all the essentials for our new place, we had each other, and that is all that mattered to me. They were safe in my arms, and I knew God would provide for us. This had been the best and most absolute splendid day I had ever experienced in my life as I lay fulfilled in overcoming my battles.

Thank You, Lord

That next morning, I let my children sleep and had an opportunity to spend quality time with them and answer any questions they had regarding their new life apart from their dad. Yet I could not miss giving God all praises that were due unto HIM. I blessed the Lord for His goodness and for His mercy keeping us safe from all hurt, harm, and danger. I praised God for allowing the four of us to be fitly joined together as one. I thanked the Lord for the fresh start in my life promising only to serve and love Him with all my soul, my mind, and my heart. I had come full circle out of a travesty that was meant to break me down; that was meant to destroy me, and my testimony. That was meant to destroy my children, God's gifts to me. My heart was grateful. My soul cried out knowing that God had been with me, and He never left me to follow anything or anyone outside His gates of protection.

Life-changing Experience

Finally, on the following Sunday, we all went to my church where I had been fellowshipping since my separation from the children. I was so happy to be bringing my children to church with me after such a long duration of being a part. I gave them a few details about the church, and they seemed excited as I did as we were arriving at our destination. As we drove up to the church, I could see their eyes were amazed while they kept asking, "mom is this the church?" When I walked inside the church with my children, I could sense their humility and wonderment as they looked around the ambiance and were met by the Lord's presence. I could see it on their little faces. My children were accustomed to being in church and visiting other churches. They were active participants in our Children's Sunday School, recreational gatherings with other children, playing the drums, you name it, they all had experience with being affiliated within a ministry before the divorce. And since I homeschooled them, I always had fun events for all the children from our old church promoting businesses involving children's education, entertainment, and networking with other homeschool moms who shared various projects.

As time went by, we settled into a good routine over the Summer. When I first started going to my new church, I purchased a CD speaking on Faith and played it often. It was an extremely popular song with a very strong message, titled "Mustard Seed Faith," (*Merritt*). When I was alone before my children began to live with me, the song helped motivate my faith in God. This song turned out to be our daily motivation throughout the week. One day while my children were getting dressed for church, I played our song. I had never heard my children really sing the song before, but this Sunday they had all started singing the song. I paused and glanced at them in their rooms singing the song while getting dressed for church. I was so impressed that these words they were singing would be living waters for them. I mean, they were singing this song with full-blown intentions, and all three of them were singing with their own style movement, rhythm, and heart expressions. I knew then that they realized this journey we were on required a strong belief and faith in God. As a result, my children began to evolve and bloom in their own way by attending their new church. We visited their grandparents every Sunday after church service, it helped them to become even more connected to family who loved them which allowed their confidence to soar as they appreciated their new lifestyle and relationship with family members. It brought happiness to their grandparents. The home I grew up in became alive with laughter and purpose. My mother was happier than I had ever seen, and my dad was proud to be an influential person significantly managing and overseeing my children's well-being in my absence. We were all together now and nothing would separate us ever again.

Interference Rises

Just when I thought I would have the peace which I created for our lives to move on, suddenly their father wanted separation between me and my children once again. They had not visited or spoken to him in several weeks. He started to interfere by questioning their church attendance. Once his thoughts settled on my attending my new church, he became intimidated, especially since he had not heard from his children in a while. I was fair in understanding his concerns, but I did not appreciate the confusion he was trying to cause within my family. He was free to plan his visits and since I had full custody, I would have been more than willing to discuss and decide on our arrangements with him. But I failed to review however was the divorce papers which included little to no payment for child support. He requested to have our children every other weekend, so they could go to his church. They cooperated with their visits with their dad, but as they gleaned from their new church and made new friends, they started to resent leaving to be with their father to attend his church. I never discouraged my children or fussed with their father about his time with them. I knew who I served. I knew all power would be restored in my hands as I continually prayed over them once they returned to me and before they left. I knew if I made it difficult for their father, he would indeed make it difficult for me, and I did not want to subject my children to our battle. Therefore, by interceding and praying for them I knew God would work things out in my favor.

The Other Woman

As previously mentioned during the time when I lived with my sister, three of my church lady friends/members came over to the house with groceries to see about me, and eventually, the four of us would often get together and have dinner. I noticed one of the ladies was always picking with her food when we came together to eat, and not adding anything to our conversation. She had not acted this way before. I knew her quite well. And on another occasion, she exhibited the same kind of behavior. I asked one of my close lady friends why the other woman was acting so odd. I commented further, "When I tried talking to her at dinner, she would shrug her shoulders, look away, or keep her head down." I could not understand why she was acting so strange. The rest of us acted normal toward each other simply enjoying each other's company. I asked again, "are you alright?" She would respond, "Yeah, I'm o.k." So, I asked my close friend this question, "Is the children's father seeing someone in the church?" My friend was somewhat hesitating, and she simply said, "let me say this if you ever want to know who the person is, ask the Holy Spirit to guide you and when you get your answer, I will confirm it with you, but just so you know, he is seeing more than one." I was even more stunned because I thought it was only one. Well after that information, I did not want to press the issue. I could not help but wander all the prospects lined up to be with my children's father. I was so peeved that I had to be connected to this man and his messiness. My concerns were this, my children: and since he was their father, I had to find a way to get him out of my business. I did not want

                                     Judah Moore

my children to be exposed to the different women coming to visit at the house while they visited him. I did not want them to be exposed to women who they were familiar with at church and who knew me. As their mother, I was not keen on them loving it up with my children when they start going to visit their father. After some time went by, I asked my sister in Christ and friend again, and she gave me the same answer. She refused to tell me who these women were. I asked my friend to explain to me her logic for not wanting to share this vital information. She claimed she did not want to hurt me. I understood that, but my rationale was if I am the one who has the right to know, then I felt the information should be given and I would handle the hurt in time. That was my rationale. I grew impatient with their father's same routine of talking with other women in the church. I started to think this was much more a significant issue for him that he was dealing with which needed professional counseling.

I decided to hold off on being too confrontational on the matter. I needed bonafide concrete evidence, and I knew God would answer me and show me the truth. I specifically wanted to know who the other woman was who had the influential persuasiveness to convince my ex-spouse to remove me out of my house causing hardships to endure a drastic change in living a productive life. God had not answered me for weeks. By this time, my children started their new elementary school experiences. My parents were helping me out financially until I was able to be interviewed for jobs. It was difficult during this time as nonprofits had not heard of Pastoral Counselors, and as a result, I dropped the title "Pastoral" and just went as "Counselor" on my resume(s). I eventually start having interviews and was able to find my first counseling occupation, along with starting a private practice.

In the meantime, I was entuned with my children's father's nuisance behaviors to have the children with him suddenly. I could not help but focus on how things suddenly changed since my children were with me now. They were in a safe and loving environment. They were not being subjected to all the confusion and mismanagement of their father's care. I knew they were in a good and stable home, so why is he interrupting how I raise our children? I really began to meditate on many different mainstreams on my suspicions. I had time to really deal with some issues that would be affecting my children. Before while I was in school, I could only pray for my children and have faith they were being cared for properly for my own sanity, which they were, but now since I was finished and moving onto employment, I had some free time to slow down and just ponder. So, I was more than ready to put the spotlight on this person. I was more shaken when I discovered who the other woman was in my ex-husband's life, in fact, the same woman who let me in my own house pretending that she was staying with the two sisters was the other woman.

One day I was prepping for a meeting and as I walk into another room in my new place, the Holy Spirit had clearly given me the first name of the other woman. I then visualize a dream I had concerning my ex-spouse him having sexual relations with a woman. I did not see her face, but this was a second confirmation of the same dream. I then contacted my closest friend who had previously instructed me to ask the Holy Spirit the name of the other woman, and when we spoke, I said to her, "is this name of the other woman, so and so?" She hesitated with sadness, and said, "yes, that's her." I could hear her hurt because she knew how much I extended my love toward her. She also shared with me other women with whom there was involvement

                                    Judah Moore

who were new members at the church shortly after my departure.

What this meant to me was that my children would be around this person often, and these women would feel like they were the mother in their lives. This entire scenario was outlandish and perverted to me. I would not have cared if he linked up with someone outside of the church who I did not know, but his involvement with women close to us and members of the church was an act of promiscuity, adultery, and misleading to the body of Christ.

Everything I had gone through in the past eight months mentally and psychologically surfaced fiercely as a desert storm. I could only see my way clear to travel over to the home where I once lived. I tried to collect myself, but my thoughts were enraged. I thought about how I spent an abundant amount of time ministering to this other woman on her spiritual growth, counseling her on keeping her own marriage intact, watching her son while she was attempting to attain her GED late in life, feeding her, and sharing my table with her almost daily. I gave quite a bit of time to her. We spent a lot of valuable time together. Never would I have thought she was scheming on working to break up our home.

I drove over to my ole house which was fifteen minutes away. I parked my car in the driveway. I approached the same side door where I was asked to leave out of almost a year ago. I did not know what I was going to do when I saw my ex-spouse. The side door was unlocked, and I walked straight into the breezeway which we had enclosed with two solid doors at each end when we initially moved in six years ago. I knocked on another door that went straight through into the kitchen. I was hoping to talk with the children's father.

One of the elderly Christian sisters who had lived with us for over ten years at different places came to the door. I told her that I needed to talk to the children's father, and I proceeded to go inside. She tried to pull the door toward her and let me know that I could not come in. She had never spoken to me in that manner. Well, I thought I could reason with her and tell her the truth about her pastor so that she could make some decisions about her membership and living arrangements. It was my deepest intent to protect her. She said to me sharply, "I love my pastor and would do anything for him." She began to justify his actions based on scripture and her belief in God. I was so shocked that she felt the way she did. I know she had always favored the pastor more than me even while living with us, and she did anything he asked her to do. And it was a noticeable difference when I encouraged us to work together. Despite how she felt toward me, I always showed her love. I never asked her to leave our house. I shared my children with her. I allowed her to serve the pastor as her occupation was as a nurse. I never interfered with her life. She mainly stayed to herself, but her sister whom I introduced Jesus Christ into her heart, we worked well together. My youngest son loved her deeply like a grandmother, and I eventually asked her to live with us a few years after her sister moved in.

I was still talking with her about my ex and when I was just about to leave, I heard the door open with the sounds of the other woman giggling. They were affectionately locked in arms as I turned around and saw them both not being bothered by my presence. My mind went blank, and everything began to move slowly. I had a flashback of the times she was present at my house when I was not at home while my children were at school. I trusted her. This was the same woman whom I asked at the dinner table if was everything all right, and she told me everything was, okay. Now I understood why she was playing in her food and not adding to our conversations.   There was instant pandemonium as my ex tried to brush past me to get into the house to protect the other woman and holding her hand. The elderly woman was still standing in the way, and I was not moving either. I tried snatching the other woman's clothing, her hair, her store mall bags, anything to do bodily harm to her, but she kept hiding behind my children's father. She was trying to find a way to escape into my house as he tried to shield her from my body movements. I kept swinging and he kept positioning his arms up and body blocking my attempts to slaughter her.

I immediately left. I did not stand around asking for an explanation "why did you do this to me with her of all people?" I had said and did enough to get my point across. I was angrier than I cared to be, and this anger had a hold on me. I was betrayed, and I felt the stabs of betrayal across my back. I could not ever do this to anyone, so why was it happening to me? I did not deserve to be tricked or lied to. My days seemed eternal. I would be reminded forever that he took her as his bride, and I had to be all right and live this decision now facing my future. I had to share my children with a vindictive woman who was so jealous of my life, that the spirit of envy stole it and claimed it as hers, and my children's father agreed with the discord.

I thought I would never see the light of day when God would grace me again with His presence to further move from under this dark cloud.

~~~
~~~

Reflecting on my future considering what happened during this season of my life, one may want to ask, "do you have any regrets about how you handled yourself with the other woman?" I pondered the thought, and I would honestly say, I have no regrets. Being so close to me as she was and then influencing and coveting all I had, with permission of course by the pastor and father of our children was a complete betrayal. I have had time through my healing to reflect on the cover-ups which tried to remain hidden. I saw where I missed things because I never imagined being betrayed by a man who I thought loved me.

As I opened my eyes during this season, I discovered women in ministry who are pastor wives are very much envied by other women in the fold. It does not matter who she is, how much she loves the church body, or how she postures herself in leadership, there will always be someone who will want to seem to be important. It is not easy becoming or being a pastor's wife, but it is vitally important that the spouse shields and protects his wife so that everyone in the body understands where his heart is. This is what the people are seeking, how much does the pastor love his wife and his children? If there is no love or consideration shown, or spoken, then the Jezebel spirit will attack.

CHAPTER THREE

"... Loved in It"

"As ye have therefore received Christ Jesus the Lord, so walk ye in him: Rooted and built up in him, and stablished in the faith, as ye have been taught, abounding therein with thanksgiving." (Colossians 2:6-7, KJV)

~~~

As I forced myself to envision and face the journey of the unforeseen crossroads of my travels through the desert sands of my life, I was facing the true realities of overseeing it alone. I suppose reality had hit me in living this life. My children had just started school a few weeks ago and now I needed to focus on a solid life plan for survival. I knew I had to attentively put myself out there. "What if I fail?" "What if I make a mistake?" All these thoughts came to mind. I had never lived so independently with dependents. It was different doing this by myself, although I had it alone when I was married. I was concerned about this type of new life I had before me alone. But I was reminded of a song that I loved to sing which I had learned at the very beginning of dedicating my life to God which spoke to my spirit. Simply saying, *"because He lives, I can face tomorrow; and I know my life was worth the living because He lives,"* (*Gaither's, 1971*). My thoughts reflected on my journey thus far and how far I had come. Jesus reminded me of all the strong people I had sitting at my table. I had developed some beautiful relationships who I knew had my back and who provided words of inspiration and motivation to me. I had a safe and secure place to live. I had the love of my parents and all my family who welcomed me with open arms without judgment; and I had the church, my spiritual family that
~~~

always offered an encouraging word unknowingly pouring into my sorrows and rebuilding hope.

On the other hand, as I continued to mature in my Christian walk, I developed an unhealthy outlook on myself. I had lost my self-confidence and disguised my appearance to be unflattering so that I would not be approached by the opposite sex. At a time when women are into their forties, they are the most confident, vivacious, and assured of their identity. For me, it was difficult to trust and uncover my past dilemmas. The few acquaintances or outsiders who I thought were understanding, when I tried talking about what I went through, asked "have you forgiven him? Have, you prayed about what you experienced?" This let me know that my situation was way over their head and too overwhelming for them to care. They did not have the empathy I so needed. I needed counsel. Someone to just hear me, and not judge whether I prayed about what occurred. I wanted to hear wisdom. Then I asked myself, why is the children's father on the phone calling me every morning? He still wanted to keep track of me. Every time I told him, I am in love with Jesus. He tried to ask a question, and every time he would get the same response until finally, finally, I mean finally, I got so tired of him calling me to check if I was with someone else, while he was married to the other woman, I said, abruptly and as rudely as I could so that he could get my point and feel the fire ignited in me, "STOP CALLING ME!!!" I sacrificed myself so that my children could have a mother in good standing with God.

I adjusted and came to terms with embracing my life as a divorced single-parent and taking charge of the responsibility of raising my children as a god-fearing woman. I would plan to raise my children as I wanted my parents to have raised me and give them love, understanding, and the support they would need to the best of my ability. I never dreamt of my life living as a divorced single parent. Not that either is disgusting, but I believed I would be married for the rest of my life and raise my children in a loving home environment. Remembering my life as a child growing up (during those porch light days) we were around other parents who were hard-working and supportive of one another. Our community neighborhood was highly energetic, full of laughter and playing with many of the kids on the street. There were a few families from Poland, White Americans that were predominately senior citizens, and mostly Black and Brown families that made up the entire cultural feel. I had come to know more about our history as I entered junior high school, and how the dynamics of our home changed after the riots during the 60s. During this time in my childhood, everyone from their respective groups got along well. Nonetheless, what I had not experienced were single moms or single mothers raising their children alone, and this was foreign to me. I instinctively decided to use my intuition and spiritual direction, plus the use of my experiences as an older sibling caring for my younger sisters when both of our parents worked full time to raise my children and believed God would direct and teach me.

My Sacrificing

I would need to further intensify my prayer life for my children because I had two sons who would need a male mentor in their life as the time approached. I knew I was not equipped to give them the face-to-face talk they would normally need, nor was I trying to compete with the paternalistic function of young boys into their adulthood. I knew I would give them all of me while guiding and teaching them to make good choices to become upstanding men, respectful to authority, and respect the opposite sex. I knew my daughter would need more protection and support, but even when raising all of them, I was always reminded by my mother that parenting does not come with a manual or a blueprint, which gave me even more respect for how she raised all her daughters.

Out of curiosity, I even purchased a popular book on, *"Help! I'm Raising My Children Alone,"* *(Jakes, 2011)*. I remember reading the book while at a doctor's appointment for more understanding, and someone there in the office laughed mocking the title out loud. Well, it did not bother me, because my mission was to gain a realization on raising my children with more spiritual knowledge and insights *"For the LORD giveth wisdom: out of his mouth cometh knowledge and understanding." (Proverbs 2:6, KJV)*.

There were many decisions I had to make as a single parent of three, and too many more decisions in the days and years to come. And because my children lived with me 100 percent of the time, I stayed on my knees. I was grateful for having my children with me and having a roof over our heads. I knew in my heart that I would be a good parent to my children because of my love for God. As their mother, I was in a fight to keep them safe. I did not want them to feel ashamed by their peers or feel left out with their father's new family, or anyone. I wanted them to know that God was their Heavenly Father and their supplier. I knew as I remained faithful and kept my relationship with God always, we would be victorious. It was my destiny to lead, train, and guide them into all truth, and I trusted God would do the rest.

As I prayerfully set up my family and position as a single parent, I decided to remain a single woman. This was

Judah Moore

an opportune time for me to discover who I was and view life with fresh eyes and learn to love myself. I had no interest in pursuing a meaningful relationship while raising my children and decided to remain celibate until I remarried again. I had a lot of internal work to do on myself. I gave further thought to keep my married last name, as I did not want to add another burden to my children's hearts. I sensed they were questioning their own identities due to the changes in their father's life, therefore I decided to carry his last name until such time. I did not want them to feel embarrassed or ashamed in having their friends or teachers ask, "why does your mother have a different last name?" I did not want to subject them to this type of questioning or the thought of trying to explain this to anyone. As I made this decision feeling this would keep my family strong, they were quite happy about my decision and appeared relieved that their identity would be intact.

Pouring and Prepping

I could see my children's confidence level being built throughout their up-and-coming years and the freedom to advance as unique individual people during their adolescence years. It was my dedication and sovereignty to surrender my entire being and life serving and worshipping God. In retrospect, this was healing for me while re-examining my life and coming to terms with my life, both past, and present. I wanted to feel that my home was a sanctuary, a secret place in building a productive life and be refreshed spiritually. I did not want to subject my children to a man visiting or coming into my home displacing and shifting authority over us. I wanted to be free to do this without hearing a male voice in my home or him persuading my love away for my children. The only voice I wanted to hear with authority was my Heavenly Father speaking and guiding me concerning all matters of the heart. Many women get caught up with persuasive decision-making choosing to become dependent on men, instead of trusting they can begin living in a whole different world toward success. Some of the fortunate ones find true love and support from an adoring partner who truly loves her and her children, and who is willing to make changes in their lives for the sake of having a desired strong union. In this case, being a single parent under the circumstances, it was wise for me to harness as much mental fortitude and succumb to my spiritual path to avoid the pitfalls of putting my children second in my life. I refused to become a statistic. Being involved intimately with a man while raising children can compromise a woman's willpower to serve and love their children unconditionally. I wanted most of all to take plenty of time to love on myself 'first' before entering a relationship. When a woman is vulnerable, I believe she should first focus on discovering herself and her purpose, so she can build a solid mindset and an appreciation for who she is so that no one can come in and push us off our square. The devil is cunning. It is hard to say what we will do and will not do when being persuaded by a man who says, "you're to be my wife" or suggest "let us move in together." This was a valuable lesson for me. This is when we should go into our prayer closet and wait for an answer from God, no matter how long it takes to receive His response. God will eventually send evidence thereof, be it an answer, a confirmation, a vision, or a dream. As we wait faithfully God will direct our path. As single mothers, we should even allow ourselves to meditate on what we received in our prayer closet before moving forward so that our foundation is solid, and our thinking is clear. As women, we need to

                                        Judah Moore

realize that the enemy wants to destroy our family(s), our children, and even the parent(s). I knew I had so much life and love to give only to my children because they gave me a reason to breathe and live. I did not have room for anyone or anything else as I focused on surviving, and to do that, I needed to put God first in every stretch of my life. Survival was my challenge every day. I knew I had it in me. Whether I was suffering psychologically or emotionally … I was determined not to give up. On days I had it rough and did not feel like getting up, I pushed myself because I had to keep our lives in order.

Thus, my days ahead continued to interfere with the battles of visitations so the children could attend their father's church.

Firmly Rooted

After my last exchange with the other woman and the children's father, within a year or two they decided to get married. I heard the news innocently come from my children's mouths. This was another slap in my face and his children. I did not respond. I wanted to hear how it affected them, as it was more important than how my children were being pressured by their father's decision. I could not believe that their father chose to make such an unorthodox and bizarre decision being he was the pastor who married her and her ex-husband years ago while we were married. I was hoping to myself that he would truly hear from God and do the right thing by waiting to marry someone else who was not close to our family. But each time my children came back home from their weekend visit with their father, the conversation of marriage arrangements intensified. I felt that their father lost his mind. I was present at her wedding and with her then-husband at the time when they got married. I was by her side.

After their wedding, my children seemed so unhappy and crushed when they returned home to me. I was grieving for them, but I knew I had something she (the other woman) did not have. I had unconditional love an exuberant amount to tend to their gifts one by one and build hope in their hearts. These spiritual gifts they possessed would be used more as they matured, but for now, they were receiving healing in their soul. They would in time eventually see it, as I transformed all the essential tools of development, they needed to make it through this hurdle. This was dysfunctional, and I understood what dysfunction was like. I had lived it throughout my teenage years and refused for my children to be in bondage by this situation. My children were not going to grow up feeling defeated by their father's decision. They would be positive influencers in society and with their walk with God by not compromising their relationships when they become older.

Build Up

From that point on, I noticed how my children were self-evolving after their father's marriage. I thank God for our church. We loved attending our new church, and we loved our pastors. There we could see and experience how our relationships bloomed and blossomed as a family. My youngest son was the first out of the children to be baptized at the church. It was a glorious moment in time. He made his own decision to give his life to Christ. This is how much spiritual impact our new church had on our lives. We were all strengthened as we faced a new circle of relationships as one. Admittedly, I had my moments of being an extreme introvert. This was not my normal personality, as I was

Judah Moore

cautious in revealing my private life. I know I missed opportunities by not being productively active in ministry in some way, as I had been at my church; but I was more entrenched in finding truth. I had been sheltered in life to a degree and I suppose what happened to me caught me off guard. I was dealing with the effects of that. I was gripped by embarrassment and shame. It was troublesome and a constant nuisance to feel this way. I had nothing to be ashamed of I know. I had not committed adultery. I had never been unfaithful. I did nothing but carry myself as a lady. For these reasons, my feelings had drawn me inward. It was difficult and awkward to be myself at times, but I managed to work through it at my pace. My children's well-being kept me from focusing on the stained spot that wanted to ruin my demeanor and confidence. So, was it a question of trusting others? I can say yes. It was such a sensitive subject for discussion with anyone, particularly if I did not know the person. And everyone is not sensitive to how you are feeling, not to mention keeping what is shared in confidence. I coped in my stillness with God and allowed Him to manage my suffering and pain. Searching for my truth, I clutched onto every new course my church offered their parishioners, such as Catechism, Understanding the Voice of God, and Understanding God & His Covenants, which were taught by a well-known missionary of a distinguished seminary school.

My Deliberation Healed

One night as many of us completed our last course, I recall carefully making my way to the other side of the church to ask our instructor and Woman of God a question after the class ended. I was thinking as she was teaching us our last portion to just ask her a question that had been bothering me since my journey. I knew the answer, but I needed to hear the answer so to remove the nagging in my mind. I trusted her to share a glimpse of what I was dealing with in my personal life. I was eager to have clarity. I knew she had the answer. I needed to hear a godly voice speak to me concerning my issue. As I hurriedly approached her before she left the building, I called her by name almost running toward her and I softly touched her for a moment on her left shoulder. I was able to get her attention. I realized it was late in the evening, so I said quickly and inquisitively asked, can I ask, "Does God approve divorce?" She hesitated and looked puzzled as to why I asked her this question. I could see in her eyes that she discerned, and then she blurted out with a voice of authority, "No" just shaking her head." She walked away. I was glad she did not ask me why. I said, "ok thank you," and stood in silence watching her as she left. I immediately felt the relief I needed to hear. I let the dust settle in my mind. I received and was free from the torment of those words which were spoken to me by my ex-husband, saying "God said you're no longer my wife." I heard the voice of the Lord God speak loud and clear. My mind was free. The word, which was spoken to heal my thoughts, I no longer had to fight in pushing those thoughts down as I now had a clear revelation. Some Christians enjoy using God's word inappropriately for justification of their own wants and needs.

Pray For Your Pastor's Wife

I crucially wanted to hear a seasoned saint, and her response, the triumphant sound, was from a warrior, an intercessory, and a praying woman. It cradled me in a place of comfort settling the very core of deceit that had me bound. That ugly slug-foot imp kept tormenting me with feelings of shame, and unworthiness, wanting me to walk away from

Judah Moore

God. I had been so accustomed to giving my life by working in the ministry of counseling, sharing, and helping women in our church when I was pastoring, that I had no one to pour into my own life. Pastor wives need ministering too. It is vitally important that the body keeps even the wife in prayer. My ministry time for myself was getting into my car and driving for a few hours playing my praise and worship music on blast, praying, and sometimes crying out to God until I felt I had a breakthrough. This was my time to be alone with God to access direction, to be strengthened, and to be loved by my Heavenly Father. I had never been confronted or experienced disrespect, lies, or deceit in a church in all my upbringing. Our church had changed so much before my departure, and I was fighting to keep it in order before things changed, not knowing I was fighting my own battle with the people the enemy used to turn against me.

New Baptism

When it was time to be baptized after we completed our final class, I was more than happy to be immersed in the water for the third time in my life. I felt this special occurrence would be quite different from any other time in my life. I walked toward the pool and the missionary, the Woman of God, the teacher, and the author of all her books on knowing God was all smiles when she saw me. I had sensed she remembered me the night after class and the question I asked her. She reached out to me gently as I came closer to the baptism pool, and she coached me down the few steps one by one into the warm water. She was full of the love and of the presence of God. This was a tender moment. I will always remember that special day. She looked at me smiling then crossed my hands over my chest and prayed the prayer of the Trinity. I cannot recall whether she laid hands on me, but as I felt myself go under the warm current of water, my feet were swishing like a fish underwater, and when she brought me up, she stood rejoicing and laughing and said: "you kicked like a fish." I nodded and happily giggled wiping the water from my face. I was so ecstatic and full of joyful tears as I stepped away never knowing whether I would see her again. I had never felt this feeling in all my times of being baptized. It was so indescribable, and believable, as it still covers me.

Profession and Calling

As I reappeared more within my life into normalcy, I discovered a rewarding occupation as a team leader in The Family Reunification Program which offered four to a maximum of six months of services aimed at working with families in which one or more children had been placed in foster care. For a family to be an appropriate referral a plan had to exist for the child/ren to be reunified with the parent within thirty days of the referral to Family Reunification. All worker teams had to be available to the families 24 hours a day, seven days a week, and my responsibility required providing a therapeutic/skill-based intervention regimen to all family members. I assisted single parents, those who were separated from their spouse, and married mothers reconnecting with child/ren before their initial court date, yet in the meantime assessing their immediate needs and working diligently in finding them adequate housing that would be safe and secure for their children. After this was complete, we used resources to locate furniture, clothing, beds, food, and other essentials before their case review. I had an opportunity to feel the emotions of so many women who had not seen their children for months or a few years. These women helped me as much as I helped them adjust to their situation giving them the hope and confidence they deserved despite their mistakes or life decisions. I helped

                                    Judah Moore

them. God gave me the words to speak into their lives within each therapy session. I could imagine deeply how they felt and as I worked through each case relationship in reunifying families, it was gratifying to see children happily living with and being with their mothers, or parents.

Before The Reunification Program, I remained in private practice and was employed within several community mental health agencies while still perfecting my therapeutic skills to further my profession serving clients experiencing major setbacks and expanding my genre and population, diverse backgrounds, and social status, ethnicity, and religion.

My calling as a Counselor centered on Christian beliefs, which facilitated in managing and promoting healthy relationships with my growing children. My career had given me a lot of insight and an appreciation for where we were in our situation. This had given me more insight into how I could further assist the mothers in their own circumstances as well. It was an honor to serve the entire family in the program. Yet, although I felt I had been shielded so much in my life, the opportunity to personally experience what these women/mothers had to go through, minus the court dates and hearings gave me fuel to ensure they were ready to face the courts' decisions. I applied this same energy to the care of my children. I prayed for them before they left for school and laid hands on them whether they understood it or not, or whether they thought their mom was overdoing it. It did not matter. I had to ensure our prayers were covered by the Blood of Jesus before they walked out the doors of our home. I was training my children to be more than ordinary, but to become conquerors. I had a desire for them to know, believe, and walk in their purposes as we meditated on the Word of God in-home and in church. I knew the enemy wants to destroy families, and with the power of God's hand upon us, this was not happening. We had family gatherings every other Friday just talking about any concerns they may have had. My floor was open for all discussions as it helped me to understand their personalities and their greatness. I encouraged them to speak and talk openly because their voice mattered and would matter in time. I did not want them to be shy in expressing themselves. This was a skill that they had to know and master to perfection, as I knew God would use them at His appointed time.

Over the years, as my children entered junior high and high school, they started to make their own decisions and choices on when to stay the weekend with their dad. I was glad that I was no longer having to hear their father's voice on the other end of the phone. I had become used to his decision and planned to never be in his presence or around him if I could help it. My children were loving their home environment and church, all their friends from school, plus they participated in playing sports, instruments, and choir rehearsals for school concerts. They were developing their own interest and multicultural community. More importantly, they were free from confusion and disappointment. When I asked them to elaborate on their reasons for not wanting to visit their father bi-weekly, it was vaguely mentioned their unhappiness with how they were being treated or poked by the other woman. I know my children did not want to tell me every detail because they knew how I felt and feared I would go over to the house again and cause a disturbance. But at some point, I decided to let it go. I had to learn how to accept their decision and resolve the matter in a different way. It angered me that she would still attempt to upset or try my children like she did when they were small. It was best for them to make the decision to choose when they wanted to visit their dad, and I continued to leave it up to them. I could tell how relieved they were to get back home after their visitations, and as a result, I found myself restructuring and remolding their personalities because they were not receiving unconditional love from the other woman.

I realized she wanted to control my children. I raised my children to respect those in authority and their elders, and although they were put in a situation as I was, they seem to manage themselves with respect around her. Moreover, the Bible speaks this, *"Thou shalt not covet thy neighbour's house, thou shalt not covet thy neighbour's wife, nor his manservant, nor his maidservant, nor his ox, nor his ass, nor any thing that is thy neighbour's." (Exodus 20:17, KJV).* The keyword is coveting. My thinking was, did she not realize that she could not be me or replace me, nor could she ever be a woman they could love like a mother because of the deception placed on them? If it were another woman in her place who my children or I did not know, this would have been a more favorable matter as I lightly mentioned before. I never discouraged my children from not visiting their father. I believe a mother or father should give their children or child the opportunity to see their parent, if able. I could have been unreasonable and very uncooperative with their father in how he ordered a divorce separating our family to be with another woman. We managed, and I can say the Lord took care of us despite the fact he was not financially able to take care of his responsibilities to ensure his children had what they needed while growing up. He again, their father left that burden on me.

Established in My Faith

Being a single parent, was a breath of fresh air. I began to feel free. I felt free. I felt stronger. I was less stressed, more relaxed, and more confident as a woman. My children were growing by leaps and bounds. By this time, we had moved into a larger apartment close to our old area. They were still able to attend the same school. What I enjoyed most was I did not have to get up early in the mornings and drive back and forth taking and picking up two or three of them to go to their different schools. My oldest son was driving now, and what a relief that was. And when they finally all went to the same school, my oldest was able to bring everyone home. What a relief. We remained a praying family before they left for school, and we continued as a family to worship at our new church as the years went by where the Lord had revealed to me in an answered prayer years ago, as God revealed to me where exactly to go and grow to further my calling and where I would receive my healing. That day will forever be etched in my heart and the entire spiritual experiences in my new church will never be forgotten.

One morning, I awakened feeling different. It was as if I was in a different body. I did not think about my situation or the life I had been subjected to as most mornings I was met with my issue. It was the after-effects of the baptism that made me feel complete. I felt like I had more clarity and direction. It was going to be a good day as I thought to myself. No more fighting those mental battles of deceit. I felt whole. I sense I had won the victory as I fought and refused to believe in the lies the enemy was trying to tell me over the years. Years of suffering and battle with depression were no more. As I sat on the side of my couch meditating on the Lord and evaluating the depths of my essence to live and not die with my head resting in my hands, I looked up and saw how bright my cozy living and dining room apartment was so bright. I loved my big windows that were side by side in separate sections of the rooms. I motioned over to the large living window overlooking the greenery as the traffic was passing by. Everything seemed purposeful. I stood there embracing the sunrays and scanning the long journeys I had endured over the past eight years as I made my way through the dusty storms and winds testing my faith. What seemed to be like an eternity was over in a blink of an eye. I praised God for taking care of me, and my children and blessing me with my family. I finally felt free, as I thought to myself. I smiled within. I was restored. I was renewed, molded, and strengthen to overcome any obstacle, because of my remarkable relationship with my God.

Finding Myself in God

All that my Heavenly Father had worked within me in my life I realized was greater accountability involving selflessness and compassion. Through it all, I had a voice and I desired to minister to others who needed to know how to walk with God trusting Him every step of the way. I had discovered my worth and the value I could share with those in need. The wilderness experience led me to uncover my spiritual identity and freedom as a unique saved woman of God with a voice to break through any barrier or obstacle that attempted to stand in my way.

Overflowing with Gratitude

Suddenly, both families start coming together to participate in my teenage children after high school activities. There were football and basketball games, musical concerts, instrumental and jazz concerts, and the sport lacrosse. I never knew when the children's father would show up, but when he did, he brought his wife. To my surprise, any awkwardness that I should have felt or any bitterness toward her was not there. I was able to communicate and talk to her as if we were still present during those times several years ago before the division started. But these were fun eventful activities, and I was so proud of my children's accomplishments. I am sure she may have thought about how I would react toward her, but God had given me a measure of compassion and love toward her. Even during the proud moments of my teens graduating, they were present at their ceremonies. Well by this time 10 years had passed by, and we had a lot to celebrate and give thanks to. I was living my life, and I was happy where I was. My children were happy. I had not been this happy in an exceedingly long time. I had a lot to be thankful for experiencing the joys of my teenagers graduating two years apart from each other, all from the same schools. I could not help but reflect on how far we had come. I thought we would continue to live a more productive life as we had all accomplished more stability in our lives.

Unexpected Transition

As I was moving forward in my career as a reunification therapist, a job opening became available to work as a manager. I applied in hopes to use their services in creating more resources for a team of therapists and their team's workers as they serviced their families. Unfortunately, I was not promoted but terminated by a newly elected manager. I did not see it coming. I had no time to prepare in restructuring my life. Again, I was pushed out. I was working on my doctorates and once this was discovered

                                          Judah Moore

on the job, I felt a swarm of enemies around me. I searched for new employment as we remained to live in our apartment. In the months ahead, I could see that we could be in trouble. I began to store everything of importance we had in public storage before they came to sit our things on the street leaving us with nothing. I evacuated the entire apartment and stayed on borrowed time. When I thought we had one last night to stay in our apartment as I was pulling into the parking lot, I and my youngest son saw two large men bringing a few essentials that we were using. On this in mid-December, so close to Christmas, we would be separated and go our separate ways once again.

I was glad I had two of my teenage children where I did not have to be concerned about how they would get to school. My youngest son would be graduating the following year. Since I had no place to live, my children had to return to live with their father once age. I was homeless in a desperate way and dropped my youngest son at his dad's. I made sure my children were situated and safe. Getting into my car and driving away in the dark of the night thinking of where I was going to lay my head was crushing and frightening. I had enough money to get a hotel room to my standards and registered at a quaint location. It was not a five-star hotel, but it appeared safe. My oldest son who was in his early twenties by now, contacted me after he got off from work. He asked where I was and came to where I was located. We sat and talked, still exalting God, and praising Him because He had worked a miracle in our life before, and we knew He would provide for us again. God had given us courage when we were afraid. He had given us peace of mind when we felt alone. Then my son began to prophesize to me that night in that hotel room as he sat on a sofa chair, and as I sat on the bed, he said, "don't be discouraged mom,

God is going to make a way for us." The words were few, but I saw a glow on him that I had not seen since he was a child preaching at the age of two. I was awe-struck as I heard the voice of God speak through him with so much authority. I was focused more on how God was using him in this hour than my predicament. Here I was with no place to live, lost my ability to be with my family, and had no idea what tomorrow would bring as to where I would go, and he was speaking with much delight that I believed even the more God would take care of me, and bring us together again.

We had (his father and I) experienced how God used our son, and how he would get up in the pulpit at the age of seven, and just start preaching. I remember when I was a lot younger, God had shown and spoken to me as a teenager while watching a televised tent revival program, that I would have a son, and he would become a powerful spirit-filled preacher from his youth. On another occasion, a traveling White Pastor from the South, who would visit our church often, and after ordaining me told me while calling my son over to us, said, "whatever your son tells you to do, do it, don't argue with him, just do it." I perceived that he meant to say when he becomes older that my son would become a man of authority preaching the Word of God. … but we both looked at each other, my son and I, and I said "o.k.," no problem, and he just shrugged his shoulders and went back to playing and socializing with the other children in the church.

Well, my oldest son left me that night at the hotel. I checked out of the hotel the next morning. I walked to my car with no idea where I was going. I started my car up. It was freezing cold. I drove out of the parking lot on a busy street having no direction. I was hungry and wanted some

                                    Judah Moore

coffee to take the edge off. I was trying the think optimistically. I was trying to stay strong and not panic. I had no more money but some spare change. I started driving North. This was all too familiar for me. This was so like my last occurrence of being displaced when my children were much smaller. As I reflected on those days, once again, I was trying to hold back my tears at the unknown before me, I said, "God help me," and I knew God heard me. I did not want to go back home and inconvenience my parents, plus I had done that too many times in my twenties. I did not want to go to a homeless shelter. I wanted to remain near my teens, and I could not imagine myself living in my car. Just when I thought there were no options for me, the Lord God Almighty spoke to me to call an admiring member from my old church. She was also a friend to the other woman. Yet this woman and I always shared words that were pleasing and uplifting. We were blessed to be in each other's company whenever we came together, and although I had not spoken to her in a few years she was my help. I immediately called her on my cell while still driving up the busy street. She answered her phone and was so glad to hear from me. I explained my situation, and she said, "girl, you better come over here, you know it's no problem. Here is my address, come right over. We would love to have you here with us." I thanked her for opening her doors and headed directly on my original path North to her place of residence.

While living apart from my teen children, I was able to find part-time work and continue with my online courses. My family and I were such a long way from each other, but they were a lot closer distance-wise than before. Their father did not reach out to me to say if you want to visit the children, feel free to come by. I had no idea as to what they were doing, but I trusted God in how they had been taught in keeping God first in their lives, and that they would continue to be respectful.

One day a friend of my youngest son's mother contacted me and revealed they were hiring in the Employment Department, and they needed Counselors/ Career Coach. I was able to start work immediately and sought to rent a house in the same district area for my youngest son to complete his last year in high school. Within those three months, while living with their father, my teenagers had gone through a life of mild changes. I was glad I was able to remove them from their dads due to our standards being different in raising our children. I knew I needed to get my children back so we could continue our journey together. I knew God had much more in store for them. Like an overly protective parent, I had to face that although it was their individual experiences, the life they had with their mother was more impressible and life-giving. I was assured that what we had gone through was a temporary setback to establish us for a continuum of blessings and no matter who got in the way to try to destroy the dynasty, we would still come out victoriously. I believe in God, and I put all my faith and trust in Him. This is what the family continued to walk in, believing in God with all our hearts, mind, and soul.

Reflective Waters

"I have planted, Apollos watered; but God gave the increase." (1 Corinthians 3:6, KJV).

In reflecting back to our previous years when my teen's started high school, I had begun pastoring a small congregation. I believed this was the direction God was

                                                                 Judah Moore

taking me and subsequently I developed many favorable relationships with other women who were called into ministry. During a span of time, I eventually merged with another church which my deceased grandmother was affiliated with located in West Virginia. My grandmother was an Apostolic preacher and affiliated with the holiness church. When she came to visit us for her revivals when I and my sister were small, she kept us in church all day and every day until she returned home. I recall the large church being so packed with women in white. My sister and I could barely move or get around. In observing these holy staunched women of God, I could sense how faithful they were about serving the Lord. My grandmother's daughter, who is my own mother also began preaching in her early teens. She told me she was 13 years old and people from all over West Virginia came back to evening service to hear her speak. She would tell me how God used her to preach on many occasions and how the people were moved by the Spirit of God in dancing and praising when she spoke. My mom would sing gospel spiritual songs by Mahalia Jackson. I grew up hearing Mahalia songs as my mother sang around the house while she was cleaning. Her favorite was "*A Rainbow in the Sky*." I recall times observing her praising God in the spirit. As a child, I did not understand, but I knew it was something within her that cause such a stirring in her spirit as I sat and stared at her as she broke out singing with joy. My mother and her sisters had a gospel singing group, and they often competed against my biological father's group traveling within their regions. My mom would say their group won most contests. When I finally met my biological father, he had revealed to me that God had called him to preach at 17 years of age, but he ran he said, and finally accepted his calling much later in life. When I visited with him and his family in New Jersey before I had children, I had the opportunity to visit his church and hear him sing. He had a powerful voice and encouraged many to give their lives to Christ. I reached out to a great woman of God in whom I inquired about putting me in contact with my grandmother's fellowship district in our area to attend church therein. My purpose for joining another church and leaving mine was to give the members a solid foundation where they could be active and partake in affiliating with others in Christ and more importantly, provide a covering for our members. We were welcomed with open arms, and we all applied ourselves within the workings and callings that God had over our lives. My three teenage children began working within the ministry. I remarried. My sons were armor bearers to the pastor for several years, along with my daughter being used in praise and worship. This was their time to share the fruits of their spiritual growth and allow the Lord to use them fully.

Apollos watered

Our third church was much closer to our home residence as the winters were so tumultuous that year. My husband and I sought another place to fellowship, and it took us a little while to find the perfect match. I felt the urgency for my teenagers to be in church. They were all out of high school now and I did not want the enemy to attempt and try to pull them into the streets. We finally found a place of interest from a weekly newspaper to worship and sought to locate it. We searched in trying to locate the church to as it was difficult to find and finally one day, we saw the church's name within a strip mall area. That next Sunday we visited and kept going thereafter. We told my oldest son first, and he seemed quite impressed as we spoke positively about the

                                                                                 Judah Moore

pastor and the services we attended for a month. Thereafter my daughter and youngest son also crossed over and our entire family was in attendance working within the ministry. My daughter continued her ministry to sing on their praise and worship team, while my youngest son sang solo parts with the choir.

My oldest had a great relationship with the pastor of the church, and he eventually, blessed my son to become the Youth Pastor. Many had coined his name "YP." This acronym was very new to me and fresh terminology. Many younger youth members admired my son and his call in serving the youth. He had a profound effectual love for his group of young people. Even the little children were calling him YP. I just giggled to myself when they called him that because I wondered if they thought that was his real (first) name. Nevertheless, it was an eye-opener to see how the children were being impacted by his teaching. If he had to work overtime on his job, the group was sorely affected by his absence, but he always found a way to make it up to them. I knew he would be doing the Lord's work soon because he exhibited the qualities of a leader and had a heart for God's people. I could see how God was molding him to be HIS own. I thanked God for giving me the gift of seeing him in a vision and knew that with all my encouraging words, prayers, and ministering, he would surrender to the calling on his life. I believed that one day his soul would be convicted, and he would pick up his staff and walk fully with God, as Moses had done. And as we continued to serve the Lord within the capacity of the ministry helping my son with special evening engagements he had for the youth, he was becoming stronger in ministering the Word of God. His appointed time was coming. I could feel it in my spirit. I did not know the time or the hour, but I knew for sure, that he would be ready.

Staying Holy

On a day that captured my attention to what God had spoken to me in the past as a teenager concerning my son being a preacher, he came to me and revealed that he wanted to talk to me about his decision to accept his calling to preach. I believe through my discussions God had been talking with him intimately for some time. He had been cleared to accept the mantle God had prepared for him. Understandably so, he was struggling with his decisions. Yet, throughout he was confident in his communications and belief to accept the responsibility to become a true disciple of Jesus Christ to preach His word. I was emotional and full of joy trying to hold my tears through his words. I reflected on the years in how we suffered from lack and how far God had brought us. I had never visualized further the bigger picture that my God had in store for us and how He would put the pieces together. I had dreamt about him speaking at churches, but as I sat and listened to my son speaking with me more about his mission and calling, I saw masses of people coming to give their lives to Christ. While we yet talked about decisions on the when, where, and how, he decided to remain at the church where we were fellowshipping until the Lord directed him further on how to move. And when it was finally time to move forward, the Pastor spoke volumes concerning my son in the festive celebration and welcoming ceremony to recognize the calling on his life. It was a magnificent ceremony, as his grandparents, friends, and the church celebrated strongly in the Holy Ghost. The pastor and friend acknowledged his responsibilities and duties and celebrated the end of his interim seasons pathing the way for a new chapter in his soon-to-be congregation's life.

As we departed ways from our third church as we waited on the voice of the Lord, my son prayerfully and diligently focused on the instructions mandated by God on how to build the church. One day, he wanted us to sit down and talk. He said, "now mom, you know dad and his wife will be coming to our church." Wait. The earth just stopped. I could not believe what I was just hearing. After my last encounter with him twenty years ago when he put me out of the house, out of the church, and would not allow me to see my children, he's coming to our church? I was enraged and stunned. I never figured them to be in our picture. I worked well with their attendance at their school activities another ten years ago, but I never imagined I would be hearing of them being a part of the church when we started. This was a different area and scenery. Based on everything which happened, was I supposed to take this lying down as if nothing ever happened to me and our family? Had I received an apology for their betrayal? Not even an "I'm sorry for messing up your life," or "I'm sorry for cheating on you with one of the members of our church?" Nothing. I could not believe they would consider showing their face without approaching me first. I tell you; I was having a real problem with this decision and my son knew it. Where had they been fellowshipping since all the members left the church after the divorce? I did not pity either of them. As far as I was concerned there were plenty of churches in the city for them to attend. They had many choices to select. Now, this was a summation of my internal thoughts. I had not expressed them at that very moment, but my son knew how I would feel about this, which was apparent as to why he wanted us to talk. He was preparing me. He knew the sacrifices I made over the years and how their lives were affected by their father's decision. He attempted to talk to me, and I tried listening. It just was not right, I said. I knew about forgiveness and repentance, but I was never confronted by those words nor given the opportunity to have closure. All these years had passed by with no communication from their father or the other woman about this matter. Yes, they both participated in my children's high school events, but this would be entirely different. Now we would be in a church body, and that would be a whole different type of accountability in all aspects. But when my son, my future pastor spoke to his mother, I tried not to hear him. I always encouraged my children to speak from their hearts and feel free to openly talk to me about concerns. I never wanted them to be reduced in conveying their thoughts. Yet, I heard him. I heard his heart speak to me. The words that followed with love. A day that I often imagined.

Aside from how I felt, I could feel Christ's loving arms embracing me, and I was open to His love for me. My Savior was aware of what I had gone through and desired to remove the old hurt that was embedded within my spirit. We may believe we are completely healed from our past until we come face to face with it and relive all the emotional pain and sadness. I thought I was completely healed. I was living for Christ and away from the pain that wanted to haunt me as I still transported it upon me. Up to this point, I felt free, and if I never saw or heard their father's name again, it was alright. The further he stayed away from me, the better. I had kept myself productively busy from my forties when this all happened and was blessed to be married in my mid-fifties, and I was happy. on Sundays, I would pour out my heart in praise and worship to the Heavens. With our upcoming conversation, I discovered that God was not

                                        Judah Moore

finished with me, and by the finish with me, I mean God was working on me. "Mom, you're going to have to open yourself to be ready to receive them, because I love my dad too," my son said, lovingly covering all the bases of our past life together as a family. Despite how things turned out between his father and me, I never taught my children to dislike their father. Although they had not agreed with his decisions, they still loved him and tried accepting her.

My son and I openly revisited the same subject matter over the course of several days and weeks. I got the impression he was assessing how well I had softened up to what I would have to accept soon when he starts having church services. And when we discussed the soon-to-be transition, my son was the one ministering to me. He would share in his conversations the Word of God which inspired me to understand how he interpreted the Word of God. What was more important was how God was using him and preparing him for ministry, respectively. We always communicated and had good talks ever since he was a child. I sensed that he was conveying that in the loss of everything we had faced and fought for to survive in the past, we still had to continue with the fact of being uncomfortable 'naturally.' I knew my son understood how I felt. He stressed his points by aligning the Word of God scripturally to our present future. He respected my feelings and let me get it all out on the table. To finish, one day my son visited me again, and in his final words of encouragement, he said to me "Jesus accepts everyone. He knows our sins, and He has forgiven all our sins." I love Jesus, and because of our last talk, I went straight to the throne room to talk with God to help me move past the chunks of pain that contributed to the non-disclosures. From that day going forward, the Holy Spirit provided the comfort I needed and miraculously worked within me. It is difficult to explain, but when you know you have taken your burdens to the Lord, you will sense a stern calmness within that has removed all those agitating disorders that are out-of-order.

Church Doors Open

Yes, the person who had wronged me, whom I bared three children for, whom I believed was a friend, partner, and supporter in our early days of marriage, was front and center with his wife at our church. I had grown spiritually. My relationships with the churches I attended over the years with my children had provided me with a place to worship the Lord in Spirit and in Truth. I was remarkably familiar with church etiquette, and more importantly, I respected authority and remained aware of the authority God had ordained me with. For me, it was not a time to joke and laugh, hold long conversations, or falsely influence the visitors. He and his wife were in God's manifested church now. I give all the glory to God for being able to raise my children in church under good teachings and fellowship among their peers. God had done this! He used me to train them and guide them in the way they should go, and that being 24/7. My prayers were answered concerning my children. Now, they were serving God and operating in their gifts and calling and loving all those who would be in attendance. I did not want their father or his wife to feel they had the privilege of being comfortable or relaxed feeling as though they could smooch with the people under false pretenses without understanding how much weight God had permitted me to share. I wanted them to feel accountable to God. I had no mercy for them, but I did have concern for their soul. And I could sense their uneasiness. I did not want his father to feel he could override our son in his ministry or the church, based on his "title." I

                                        Judah Moore

was protecting my son and the vision that God had imparted to him before we opened the church. Yet, each Sunday became natural as we all came to worship together with the entire body of believers. Over the years, we co-habituated well and became accustomed to each other's presence. Communicating at length was often avoided. I had thought within the first year that an apology or asking for forgiveness should have occurred, but it never happened. We were going into four years, and still no accountability for the fiasco they both created in my life, and his children.

Deception and Forgiveness

I was given a luxurious opportunity by one of our church members, who is dear to my heart, to go on a cruise. I was hesitating as this was a first for me to be on the seas for several days. I soon discovered that the other woman would be traveling on the trip as well, and it was recommended that we be roommates. I had silently given this much prayer and thought. I felt this could be a break and it would finally bring us together. No one in the church knew of my story. I had imagined us having the freedom of talking freely. The thought refreshed me. I could finally have closure as I deeply wanted a resolution to this issue discussing honestly the why's, the how's, and the reasons for doing what she did. It was my desire to move on so that I could finally have a passage into a new life. I imagined that after our conversation, we would pray together and have expressive words of forgiveness and understanding. I believed that God would do something special in her life after we prayed together. I wanted the absolute best for her life also.

The day for departure finally came. There was a distance between us and avoidance in recognizing my presence by the other woman. I took it in stride. We boarded the plane to our destination, and her seat was in front of me. I enjoyed the flight, especially flying above the clouds. I always feel closer to God up there being above the clouds and scanning all of His wondrous beauty as I am seeking, meditating, and communing my spirit with God, oh so majestic! Since I had the window seat, the person sitting next to me wanted to know if he could take pictures of the heavenly landscape. Not a problem I responded, so I moved back as he took it all in. As this was taking place, I felt a pit in my stomach. God quieted me as I was able to discern conversation about me. I lend forward a bit to see where the other woman was sitting and saw two heads together whispering back and forth. I did not even realize she was sitting in front of me. How could I have missed that I thought? I brushed it aside and did not think any more about it. Once we all arrived inside the terminal at the airport preparing to find a bus to take us to the ship, I was asked by one of our church members if I would not mind switching roommates. I was shocked. I did not want to reveal to her the real reason for the switch, nor did I want to take my anger of disappointment out on her. She was close to me, and she had no idea about my story or my history with this other woman. But I was sorely disappointed. I held my emotions at bay as I surveillance the audacity and trickery of this entire request made by the other woman. She stabbed me in my back again. I knew she created this scheme. I was feeling very bitter. I did not want to fully disclose how I was feeling about her request, as my bitterness was not toward her who asked me to switch. She had no idea why she was coaxed into this request. I agreed to the switch. As we all began to walk through the airport, my carrying all my luggage, I tried hard to work through the deception which insulted my

                                          Judah Moore

intelligence. Here I was again having to feel "put out," and so far away from home. I had traveled and come too far in my personal and spiritual life to be dismissed. I had no way of canceling this trip. I had no interest in going any further. So, I had to pray, pray that my emotions be settled. I prayed and asked God to help me be in Him and continue to be used as a light for someone who needed to know Him in a special way.

A few days had gone by. I was winging my enjoyment. I had no interest to be with anyone. I just wanted to stay to myself. The only time I fully enjoyed myself during those first few days was dressing up, going to dinner, and sometimes participating in Karaoke. Since I was rooming with a teenager, often her young friends or family members start coming to the room asking for her, and she was always gone enjoying herself. To my surprise, when they came to the room and saw she was not available, they would ask if they could spend time together with me and talk. And this happened on a few occasions. I was open and welcomed it with open arms. I asked myself sort of chucklingly to myself why they would want to talk with an older woman when they could be enjoying so many activities, they had available on the ship. Well, we talked about anything that was of interest to them. I let them guide the conversation. I was open and receptive to their presence. I was there to give them words of encouragement; anything positive to enlighten them to grow further in their maturation.

On the following day, one of the young ladies came back to visit, and brought someone else with her to the cabin, again looking for my roommate. They did not seem to be bothered that they had missed her again. But they asked if they could come in, and I said "sure." They came in and made themselves comfortable. Our conversations were light in the beginning and before I knew it, I began to speak to them about God and asked had they ever considered how spiritual images show up in the clouds with many different imageries. They were impressed by this knowledge. At first, I was concerned that I had given them too much information that they would not fathom. They could not contain themselves. One of the young ladies said she has seen the same thing but had never imparted the depths of the spiritual closeness to God. They were so excited, and I looked at them with a surprise look, as the other young lady stated, "I have seen that before and would see angel forms in the clouds." They began to talk about the Titanic. One of the young ladies mentioned how beautiful it was at the very top of the ship. Oh, WOW I thought to myself. I had turned child-like suddenly. I asked them, "would you mind showing me how to get to the top of the ship?" They both said, "not at all, we'll take you, let's go!" We left the room, and I could tell they were as happy about going to the top of the ship as I was while we walked down the hallway. Finally, once we had surpassed a long walk to get to the first layer of stairs, one of the young ladies held my hand to ensure my climb was secure as we went up the steep stairs. They reminded me of my own daughter. Her cousin was right behind me, making sure I did not fall as we got closer to the top deck. We still had a way to go as we crossed over to another part of the ship, getting closer to the ship's stern. And as we walked toward the very end of the ship, finally reaching the edge at the top, I could see the sea for miles and miles ahead of us. We knew we were in the presence of God. We were astonished by all the wonderment. The sound of the ocean's deep waves, the evening winds, the movement of

                              Judah Moore

the ship, and the enormous interface facilitating God's creations all moved me. We were standing next to each other as if we were inextricably linked. I started to search for images in the cloud, just like I used to do as a child while lying on the grass in my backyard. When I was about six or seven years old, my Sunday school teacher use to teach his class about how God's images can be seen in the clouds. And then one day, I tried it, looking up at the clouds seeking God the best way I knew how. This was a way of life for me back then and has remained my way of hearing from God still today. So, I started the conversation and gave spiritual perceptions on a few clouds and asked for their feedback on what they saw. They began to share and ask questions about certain cloud forms and imaginaries that were before us. I shared with them my insight as they gained several insightful awareness to their questions. They began to explore for themselves. I was glad to see that because each of us needs to know the special workings of God. We stood close to each other as the winds continue to blow on us as the ship took on the massive waters set before us. We were just relaxing, sharing, and pointing at the different clouds as they set in motion to take on different shapes, expanding in and out, forming, separating, and coming together continuing in many configurations and shapes. I noticed the young ladies began to venture out by themselves as we stood there at the top of the ship discussing the cloud formations and images. While they were conversing and sharing their thoughts with each other, I slipped away into my thoughts meditating and focusing in on the immense vision of the massive and magnificent beauty of God's creations. The deep blue waters were choppy and flowing with rhythm and never-ending as my eyes searched for land around us. The sky's radiance revealed an assortment of colors that interacted with each segment of the earth giving it rain to the west and the dawn of the evening to the east. There in the center far ahead was a bright rainbow light from the evening rays setting glowing in the sky while the clouds around it looked like storm clouds on each side of us. I had to reflect a minute. It was getting late and wanted to stay if I could. But as I reflected on the ubiquity of God's foundation and formations, I turned to my friends and began to minister to them on the wonderful things of God, and ways of talking and conversing with Him at any time to gain total access to His presence because He will reveal much to those who have an ear to hear. They listened intently as we looked at how the sky and clouds were coming even more into the evening. We decided to end our moments of 'awe' and returned to our separate suites. As we walked back to our rooms, we were quiet and bursting spiritually from our venture. I was full, invigorated, and thankful to God to of had the occasion to teach and share His goodness so they will let their light shine all in due time.

When I returned to my cabin I start packing. I was ready to return home to the people who loved me, my husband and family. I could not help but reflect on what could have been between myself and the other woman if we did have a heart-to-heart conversation. I was so looking forward to making amends and finding closure on this matter of deception with my children's father disrupting all our lives. This was an added purpose for my travels so we could move forward. Surely an opportune time to freely talk. Of course, I could have approached her, yet I knew she would have avoided me as she is not good with confrontation. At some point in our Christian walk, we must accept responsibility for our sins and faults (*Proverbs 28:13, NIV*). To mask or avoid a situation will only prolong our spiritual growth. To continually step over an issue and sweep it under the rug to keep it covered will only stagnate us and grieve the Holy Spirit. We should ask ourselves is it better to confront what I did head-on with a repented heart, or let God chastise us for our sin? I would rather come face to face with the issue than be chastised by God. I know what being chasten feels like. God forgives those who ask for forgiveness and releases us back into His hands because we have surrendered ourselves to His perfect will. From that point, God will use us, deliver us, cause us to be sensitive to others, fuel or restore our calling, and use the testimony of our sin and wrongness to share without shame to those who will benefit from our testimony into deliverance (*Acts 3:9, NIV*).

No doubt once my feet hit the soil of my homeland, I was grieved to have this burden still upon me, and still around me. My spouse embraced me as he knew how I felt. Even my son was expecting good news that we would be facing a different kind of union once matters were resolved, but the news gave no joy only heartache. His soul was grieved as he hoped there would be a coming together between us, yet he encouraged me as he knew over the course of twenty years or more, I had sacrificed and continued to love her as a sister in Christ. I received his words of encouragement as he hugged me with my commitment to remain steadfast to the calling of my life with even more boldness and love.

‎

CONCLUSION

I was getting ready for church one Sunday morning when I felt such a strong connection to the Lord. On Sundays, I am overly sensitive to God's presence, as I maximize my spirit-man to be open to His direction in how He may want to use me. My main desire, which I expressed to God, was to have closure in my relationship with the other woman. It was clear to me that she would never go out of her way to speak with me beyond a simple "hello." And no amount of small talk I made with her resulted in a more intimate conversation. This was before she became ill. She developed a severe illness after my husband died. She was able to return to worship service within a few months. My thoughts and prayers were with her, and I frequently inquired about her condition as she improved.

As I finished getting dressed, the closure stayed with me. But I had a feeling God was going to do something about it. My spirit was open and willing to be used in whatever way He saw fit. As we approached our church, I felt the presence of the Holy Spirit, and as my daughter sang in our praise and worship service, I went to the altar and prayed there. God's spirit was heavy, and I remained composed in the heaviness as we went through the first service to the end, waiting to hear God's voice. At the end of the service, I remained seated, contemplating how I would approach the other woman to amend everything and have the freedom to move on into the fullness that God desired for me. "Mom," my son's voice said calling out to me. I turned to see him standing with the other woman, his father, and a deaconess. He motioned for me to come over to where they were with his hand. My pastor began speaking to us as soon as I walked over to the other side of the sanctuary where they were standing. I knew exactly what God was preparing me to do at this point. The pastor spoke with authority and with conviction to resolve this issue and seek God's forgiveness. He continued to speak as I received all which was spoken, and then I recall him saying to her, "now (Pastor, called my name) is going to lay hands on you and ask God's healing concerning your illness," and he walked away.   I immediately touched her ailing body full of sicknesses, both mental and physical as she cried out giving God praise. Both the deaconess and her husband were standing her up as she was already weak in her body before I prayed over her. As I finished praying for her, she said to me, "I love you so much." I sensed God was sharing with me that this was her apology. I could feel deep in her fragile body and her tight grip of my hands that she sincerely meant it, and I received. We hugged, and she turned to her husband for support, hugging him as he pulled me in for a three-way embrace while he was praising God. I walked away with the closure I so deserved, knowing that the peels and layers would easily fall off, and this was a good start.

Jesus said to him, "Get thee hence, Satan: for it is written, Thou shalt worship the Lord thy God, and him only shalt thou serve. Then the devil leaveth him, and behold, angels came and ministered unto him." (Matthew 4:10-11, KJV).

What we fail to realize, if we are holding unto unforgiveness it is not possible to experience God's love or even act upon it. Jesus Christ is the highest epitome of LOVE. He died for our sins because He loves us. He sacrificed His life because He LOVES us. He takes our intercessions to the Throne of Grace because He loves us. He intercedes for us because HE LOVES us. He sent us the Comforter that being The Holy Spirit because He loves us.

                                          Judah Moore

He has equipped the saints with gifts and talents that breaths upon us by the Holy Spirit for the glorification of God to heal, set free and deliver those who yearning forgiveness, deliverance, joy, and happiness, because He loves us. Jesus did all of this for us because HE loves his Heavenly Father, and His Father loves his Son, and we are loved. Our Savior sits beside us when we are lying in a sick bed. He sends the/our heavenly angels that worship and bow at the throne of God all day, uninterrupted, ceaselessly, continuously to watch over us when we are faced with unpredictable circumstances, hardship, and miseries.

Jesus Christ surrender His life and humbly took on the assignment to be tempted by the adversary knowing He (Jesus) had all power in His hands. Our Savior knew that His Heavenly Father was covering Him as He accepted the commission to be tempted to fulfill God's promises on all our lives. After all the coercion, tempting, flattering, convincing, and intimidating to cast doubt on Jesus' call to the world, in that wilderness, the adversary knew in its deceitfulness of false promises to Christ in the wilderness, the adversary had not won rule over us. When we are backed up against the wall, we must fight back with the Word of God and His promises over us. We must put on our warrior shield of faith and slay that Goliath as David did ... fight back and do not take the punches that the enemy wants us to bow too or feel. The devil was not going to have my mind, or my children. I fought back. I was in a fight to save my life. I was in a fight of determination to get my children safely in my arms, and that took fasting and praying. Although I was aware of my anointing and call on my life, I prayed and sought God to send me to a strong church that was delivering the pure Word of God and that operated in all things in decent and in order. I was not going to stop attending church just because I was no longer invited to attend a church that I helped build. Although we may feel like quitting, do not quit. You have the words to speak up to your Heavenly Father to get that enemy off your back, and if you believe in speaking in tongues, put that language on the problem. It confuses the enemy. It has no way to enter in upon your prayer request that you have given to your Savior Jesus Christ. You are, we are, all of God's people are covered by the Blood of Jesus, therefore speak the anointed Word of God, and make it plain.

I want to emphasize that if you are having an unusual wilderness experience, do not complain or murmur. You must understand that God is doing something BIGGER in your life, and He is preparing and prepping you for abundant and unlimited blessings. Even though the enemy was out to destroy me during this experience, God preserved me for His perfect will to be on my life. God kept my mind from spiraling into unstable emotions. I was not swallowed in a quicksand. I was not amused with mirages. The enemy hoped I would surrender and compromise the calling on my life. God kept my thoughts from rocketing into a deep depression and suicidal thoughts, as the enemy tried tricking Jesus by saying *"If thou be the Son of God, cast thyself down: for it is written, He shall give his angels charge concerning thee: and in their hands they shall bear thee up, lest at any time thou dash thy foot against a stone. Jesus said unto him, it is written again, thou shalt not tempt the Lord they God."* *(Matthew 4:6-7, KJV).* In Jesus' weaken physical and mental state, the enemy was encouraging Jesus to give up, to die, to harm himself. Therefore, we must keep our minds and hearts stayed on Christ Jesus. Often, we think we are by ourselves, but the greater one that lives on the inside of us is beckoning us to call on Him and trust the process of being loved in the tribulation. God kept me from disappearing and abandoning everyone who cared about me. I am thankful I went back home to see my parents. There was the love I needed. I had been separated from my parents intentionally because of one man who did not want me to have relationships with my mother and all those who loved me.

I will never know why the children's father chose to end our relationship on the day he kicked me out of the house that night, as I close my memoir. I only know that when a man reacts like that, it's usually because he is having an affair with someone other than his faithful wife. Nonetheless, I have grown in my relationship with my Savior, Jesus Christ, the only one who loves and can love me unconditionally. I pray that your walk of embrace be eminent as you give glory to our Heavenly Father as you faithfully stride with the Trinity that encompasses all you will ever need to *Loving Who You and Being Loved In it*.

ACKNOWLEDGMENTS

God answered my prayer by leading me to a church that preached the Holy Spoken Words of the Bible, quenching my thirst as I journeyed through the wilderness. Bishop Andrew and Viveca Merritt, the founders of Straight Gate International Church, are blessed and honorable servants of the Lord. Thank you for imparting me and my children with the eternal memories of praising and worshiping God because of your heartfelt ministry; and many blessings for your compassion for God's people.

~~~

After many years apart from my parents, I was blessed as a prodigal daughter to have their armor cover me during my return home while my children were separated from me. My father is no longer with us, but I am grateful that he went into the enemy's camp to keep an eye on them and ensure their well-being was secure during my brief absence. Thank you, especially, to my sister Lori for her love and hospitality.

~~~

God has blessed me with some wonderful friends, and I want to acknowledge a special person who has always had a special place in my heart. Leslie Tillman, you have always been truthful and honest with me as I served as your pastor. You do not find many parishioners as yourself. Thank you for sharing with me the truth, even when it hurt and grieved my spirit. I appreciate you so much.

~~~
~~~

I want to say thank you Lori McLaughlin and Marilyn Taylor for providing shelter and blessing me with your humility and hospitality.

~~~

Thank you so much, Linda Ross. Not only with the book, but also with the unexpected death of my husband. When I was weak and unsure what to do, you were brave for me. Your efforts as mistress of ceremonies at the homecoming were much appreciated.

~~~

Cheryl Preston–Gomez, my best childhood friend. Your initiative and determination in facilitating a GoFundMe page for my deceased husband's burial was greatly appreciated. Thank you for your love, kindness, and friendship.

~~~

Thank you very much, dear cousin. Robin Cage, you are the only voice that can propel me forward, you're my big sister for sure! When I called and was feeling defeated and uninspired, you lifted me up as you always have done since our childhood. It took only your six words, and I was on it. That was it, and I got busy. Love you.

~~~

And finally, to my always beloved "suga bear" of the last ten years, you had always told me, "Honey, God has given you the gift of writing," and you continually inspired me to finish this book and not stop. Thank you for your strength and character, love, and wisdom.

Judah Moore

ABOUT JUDAH MOORE

Intuitional Transformational Coach, Freelance Writer, and Speaker

Judah Moore is a talented freelance writer who writes articles for cosmetic and esthetic surgery professionals, as well as healthcare, business, and economics. She has written two anthology stories published by Habakkuk Publishing: "Shine: Hidden No Longer," and "It's Possible: Living Beyond Limitations!" She has been ordained and anointed by God to transform the lives of many people so that they can reach their full potential and destiny. She received her Life Coach certification from The Institute for Life Coach Training, as well as a double master's degree in Pastoral Counseling from Ashland Theological Seminary and Capella University in Management of Leaders in Nonprofit Organizations. She attends Greater City Church, where her eldest son is the Founder and Pastor.

Judah is available to provide professional services in consulting, coaching, and private counseling. She is available for speaking engagements.

Email requests to: moore.of.judah@gmail.com.

Thanking you for your support. I pray the words that flowed across the pages blessed and healed your heart with the precious Blood of Jesus' Name. Amen.

BIBLIOGRAPHY

Barna, G. (n.d.) *African Americans and Black Community.*
https://www.barna.com/about/george-barna/
http://www.healthymarriageinfo.org/research-
policy/marriage-facts-and-research/marriage-and-divorce-
statistics-by-culture/african-americans-and-black-
community/

Gaither's, (1971). Official video for *"Because He Lives."*
[Live] feat. Gaither Vocal Band Download on iTunes here:
https://itunes.apple.com/album/billy-graham-music-
homecoming/id...
https://www.youtube.com/watch?v=2Oz_caE8oQE.
(Written by: Gloria Gaither, William J. Gaither).

Gruits, P.B. (1985). *"Understanding God and His
Covenants."* Peterpat Publishing.

Jackson, M. (℗ Originally released in 1959). *"God Put A
Rainbow in the Sky."* All rights reserved by Columbia
Records, a division of Sony Music Entertainment.
https://youtu.be/dOFP-82B5NQ

Jakes, T.D. (2011). *"Help! I'm Raising My Children
Alone: A practical guide to bringing up happy, healthy kids
on your own."* (Publisher).

Lyons, M.J. (2017/04/25). *"Under Spiritual Arrest."*
https://thykingdomcomeinc.wordpress.com/2017/04/25/und
er-spiritual-arrest.

Merritt, A. (2000). *"Mustard Seed Faith."* Bishop Andrew Merritt and The Straight Gate Mass Choir.
Canción: Mustard Seed Faith, Intérprete: Bishop Andrew Merritt, Album: Faith in The House, Compositor: Steven Ford. (c) 1984 Integrity's Hosanna! Music.
https://youtu.be/8nj9gyd301c
https://www.youtube.com/playlist?list=OLAK5uy_kf6Cx7ncG2-6Lc2UWAFc-qbl0OFbGOwJY

Merritt, V. (1997). *"Lord, Arrest Me."* (Prayer audio recording). Straight Gate 2014 International Church. https://straightgate.net/.

                                                          Judah Moore

RESOURCE

Centers for Disease Control and Prevention
https://www.cdc.gov/suicide/resources/index.html

* 9 7 9 8 9 8 6 5 8 0 7 1 5 *